*Rob Ganley*

# 111 Places
# in Coventry
# That You
# Shouldn't Miss

*Photographs by Ian Williams*

T0150548

emons:

For Anna and Sue, Joe and Iris
Thank you for looking after us –
we couldn't have done this without you.
*Rob Ganley & Ian Williams*

MIX
Paper from
responsible sources
FSC® C043106

© Emons Verlag GmbH
© Photographs by Ian Williams
© Cover icon: mauritius images/Charles Walker Collection/Alamy
Layout: Eva Kraskes, based on a design
by Lübbeke | Naumann | Thoben
Maps: altancicek.design, www.altancicek.de
Basic cartographical information from Openstreetmap,
© OpenStreetMap-Mitwirkende, OdbL
Editing: Martin Sketchley
Printing and binding: Grafisches Centrum Cuno, Calbe
Printed in Germany 2021
ISBN 978-3-7408-1044-3
First edition

*Did you enjoy this guidebook? Would you like to see more?*
*Join us in uncovering new places around the world on:*
*www.111places.com*

# Foreword

Coventry is home to around 400,000 people, whose heritage lives on in its architecture and art, from its visionary centre to its outlying estates. In this book we've tried to capture the city's character through the stories of its unique but perhaps lesser-known places.

The difficulties of 2020 couldn't dent the enthusiasm of the Coventrians we spoke to. We'll share their passion for everything from artisan brewing to the history of watchmaking, from producing theatre in art deco surroundings to a shrine to Phil Silvers. We'll reveal Coventry's major medieval influence, and an industrial heritage from cloth-making to becoming an engineering powerhouse producing cars and bicycles. Indeed, the production of munitions made Coventry a prime target in World War II, resulting in the Luftwaffe flattening its medieval heart – and thus influencing its appearance today, as the city emerged from the ashes of the Blitz.

We'll cast light on a quirky homage to Lady Godiva, and the origin of the phrase 'sent to Coventry'. We'll reveal the significance of the elephant on the city's coat of arms and the crest of Coventry City FC, and its inspiration for architects. We'll explore the influence of Coventry's long roll call of homegrown stars, from *Man Like Mobeen's* Guz Khan, to Bhangra star Panjabi MC, rap artists, actors and inventors, politicians and sporting stars, to the impact of being awarded UK City of Culture status. As well as locations such as the city's cathedrals and boho FarGo village, we'll help you find gems including the largest bookstore in the region, the origins of the 2-Tone music scene, and George Shaw's paintings in the Tile Hill area.

For me, writing this guidebook has been a nostalgic and inspirational journey. I hope it reads as it is intended – a heartfelt tribute to the city of my upbringing – and that you, too, find inspiration in its pages.

# 111 Places

# 1__2-Tone Village and Café

*Wonderful evocation of Cov's coolest era*

The 2-Tone Village occupies a courtyard between the main Walsgrave Road through Ball Hall in Coventry's Stoke area, and the Marlborough Road side street. It's a wonderful and unique tribute to the ska-based music phenomenon that emerged from Coventry in the late 1970s and became a national movement, largely thanks to 2-Tone Coventry bands The Specials and The Selecter.

2-Tone was a mix of Jamaican ska with new wave and even punk music, and took its name from the record label founded in 1979 by Jerry Dammers. Dammers was also a founding member of The Specials, which had UK chart hits with *Too Much Too Young*, and *Ghost Town*. 2-Tone also reflected a message of racial integration, with a mix of black and white performers in the most popular bands of the movement, plus cutting-edge styling such as the Walt Jabsco logo featuring a man in sharp 2-Tone clothing that became the movement's icon.

The village started out as 2-Tone Central – a museum, café and club – in October 2010, before relocating to its current site in August 2011. Today, the line-up of shops that comprise the village includes the award-winning 2-Tone Café and Simmer Down Caribbean Restaurant, the 2-Tone Corner sub-culture shop, selling fashion gear and accessories, and the Hall of Fame memorabilia store, offering signed records, CDs, books, pictures and collectables. There's also the Coventry Music Wall of Fame, the Coventry Music Museum (see ch. 24) and Knights Bar, which offers regular live gigs, DJs and music nights. There's great attention to detail throughout: in the café, a black and white mural of key 2-Tone performers is covered with signatures, with black and white furniture and signature check pattern unmissable. In Knights Bar the ceiling artwork is a giant record, the floor a chessboard. It's a wonderfully friendly and celebratory place for any music fan to spend some time.

Address 74–80 Walsgrave Road, CV2 4ED, +44 (0)24 7767 1242, www.2tonevillage.com |
Getting there 7-minute ride on the 9 bus from Pool Meadow station | Hours Café,
restaurant and bar, plus courtyard displays, Wed–Mon 8am–6pm | Tip Just a 5-minute
walk away is Alpha House in Barras Heath. This 17-storey tower block was the world's first
building to use the 'Jack Block' construction system in 1963 – that is, the roof and top floor
were built first at ground level, then 'jacked up' as other floors were built beneath.

# 2 22 Bayley Lane

*Characterful cottage opposite the Old Cathedral*

22 Bayley Lane was constructed around 1500, and is the only surviving example of its type in an area that, until World War II, was densely packed with such characterful buildings. The timber-framed cottage is at the heart of Coventry's Cathedral Quarter, and just a few steps away from the Old Cathedral's ruins. It's understood to have been one of a row of similar cottages when constructed in the 16th century. These included 23 Bayley Lane, next door, although the latter was re-fronted in the late 18th century.

Number 22 is most distinctive for its original carved and traceried woodwork, and its black-and-white frontage. Among the eye-catching woodwork at street level is a distinctive carved corner post, which features a series of miniature Gothic church windows. This post, to support the wall and upper floor, along with the decorative wooden gable barge boards, were designed by the great Victorian architect Augustus Charles Pugin in the early 19th century. The cottage's brick chimneys were added in the 17th century, and its main shopfront windows were added in the early 19th century. While the ground floor has modern red-brick in-filling, the upper floor features diamond paned glass, exposed timber framework, white-painted plaster in-filling, and is jettied out part way over the cobbled street below. There are black wooden entry doors on the front and gable aspects, each beneath a pair of triangular corner spandrels, with decorative detailing. The building was once connected to the adjacent St Mary's Guildhall by a first floor extension on the gable end of the building where this extension would have been located.

Over the last couple of centuries, 22 Bayley Lane has housed bakers, the verger of St Michael – the Old Cathedral opposite the house – and more recently a firm of solicitors. A recent proposal to turn it into student accommodation was unsuccessful.

Address 22 Bayley Lane, CV1 5RJ | Getting there 13-minute walk from Coventry railway station via Hertford Street, or 5-minute walk from Pool Meadow bus station | Hours Only viewable from the outside | Tip 50 metres away is Drapers' Hall, a wonderful, 1830s' Regency building in Greek Revival style. It houses a splendid ballroom, and is undergoing restoration at the time of writing.

# 3 Allesley Walled Garden

*Showcasing organic horticulture from 200 years ago*

The Allesley Park Walled Garden Group was started by volunteers in 1997, with a plan to restore and recreate a kitchen garden as it would have looked some 200 years ago. Using old varieties of flowers, fruit and vegetables, and traditional organic methods of horticulture, it's a great example of the type of planting seen in 18th-century Georgian estates.

Back then, Allesley Hall was owned by John Neale, Lord of the Manor and High Sheriff of Warwickshire. Neale had a keen interest in growing vegetables, fruit and flowers, and for the next 150 years the garden produced food, herbs and flowers for the Hall's occupants. It sits within Allesley park, which was a deer park in medieval times, with the original walls dating from around 1785. They were built using handmade bricks, with lime mortar, and are between eight and 14 feet in height.

By the late 19th century the garden included a range of cold frame greenhouses, such as a vinery and stove house, forcing pits and potting sheds, and an orchard. The present Allesley Hall was built in 1909 for the Iliffe family. After 1937, when the Hall and its park were given by Lord Iliffe to the people of Coventry, the walled garden was used to raise bedding plants. In the 1960s it was landscaped as an ornamental garden with wall shrubs, rose beds and island beds.

Today, the volunteers work with schools on horticulture and wildlife projects, as well as welcoming visitors. A quarter of the 1.5-acre site has been planted with vegetable beds, flower borders and fruit trees, and there's a market on the third Saturday of each month selling produce from the garden. Volunteers are happy to talk about everything from box hedging, carpets of wildflowers around the fruiting trees, to making compost in the traditional way, and much more, and often deliver events such as organic gardening demonstrations.

**Address** Allesley Hall Drive, Allesley, CV5 9AD, +44 (0)24 7640 2030 | **Getting there** 15-minute ride on the X1 bus from Pool Meadow station | **Hours** Daily 10am–midday | **Tip** Also located in Allesley Park is a popular pitch and putt golf course and children's play areas.

# 4 Arden House in Allesley
*Red-brick home to an unsung local hero*

This home in the pretty village of Allesley is a three-storey, Grade II-listed house set back from the road behind ornamental railings, and dates back to the 18th century. It was formerly the residence of Dr Margaret Mitchell, a woman who led a fascinating life. Today it's a private residence, so is not open to the public.

Mitchell began her career as a doctor in the Coventry and Warwickshire Hospital casualty department, and became a specialist in treating eye diseases. The Coventry Society reported that for her services as a volunteer with the Red Cross in France, at the age of just 22 she was awarded the Croix de Guerre – a French military decoration given to foreign military forces allied to France during World War I for acts of heroism. In the 1920s, she became a medical missionary in the Himalayan Kingdom of Kashmir while it was still part of the British Empire. Before the outbreak of World War II, she went to Persia to lead a mission hospital. Other countries she visited in a medical capacity included the Philippines, Thailand and India.

When she returned to live in Allesley she set up a first-aid post in the village. Mitchell was also President of the Women's section of the Royal British Legion, the Armed Forces charity, and organised Coventry's Poppy Appeal for over 40 years. She also helped raise funds for a Christian Medical Hospital in Southern India. Throughout the 1950s and 1960s she dedicated herself to the cause of women, as secretary of the Coventry branch of the National Council of Women (NCW), which sought improvements in the welfare of women and children. As a member of the International Association of the NCW, she travelled to Helsinki, Canada, Turkey and Russia. Indeed, it was during a trip to Persia in May 1966, as a delegate to the triennial conference of the International Council of Women, that she suffered a heart attack, and later died at her home on 1 January, 1967.

Address 74 Birmingham Road, CV5 9GX | Getting there 15 minutes on the X1 bus from Pool Meadow station | Hours Only viewable from the outside | Tip Pretty All Saints Church in Allesley Village dates back to the 13th century and is Grade I listed. It's just a 2-minute walk away.

# 5 Astley Book Farm
*Cathedral of calm for bookworms*

A track off Astley Lane, located in pretty rolling landscape just to the north of Coventry, leads to red-brick barns, within which is a remarkable bookshop. It's the largest second-hand book shop in the Midlands, home to around 80,000 titles ranging from rare and out-of-print books, antiquarian and valuable collectables, to a vast display of fiction and non-fiction titles. Shelves and bookcases form a maze, and there are nooks, crannies and cosy reading corners at every turn: cushions on windowsills, comfy leather sofas around a wood burner, a delightful children's hayloft for kids to browse, plus a 'Ten Bob Barn' packed with books for 50p. And dotted between the shelves or perched on beams are quirky and artfully mounted signs and trinkets, lovingly collected and displayed.

Co-founded by owner Vivienne Mills, Astley Book Farm is located on Arbury Estate, home to Arbury Hall, family seat of Lord and Lady Daventry. Mills moved into the rundown farmhouse in the early 1990s, and set about breathing new life into it and the connected barns. Because George Eliot had been born on the estate back in 1819, and several of her novels are set in the Warwickshire countryside of her youth, it was considered a promising literary connection for a bookshop.

By 2004 Mills had filled one barn with books and opened for business – the other barns followed over the years. As well as all the books there's a lovely café serving locally baked cakes and bread, sandwiches, coffee, wine and beer. There's also an outdoor courtyard with tables and chairs for al fresco lunches. It's a rural destination, but the bookshop is notable for how beautifully and meticulously presented everything is – there's not a dust mote or whiff of musty books to be found. Just as impressive is its commitment to being open almost every day of the year – Astley Book Farm is truly a paradise for book-lovers.

Address Astley Lane, Bedworth, CV12 0NE, +44 (0)24 7649 0235, www.astleybookfarm.com |
Getting there Best visited by car, with plenty of on-site parking. For public transport, take the
55 then the 79 buses towards Nuneaton from Pool Meadow station, then a 30-minute walk |
Hours Daily 10am–5pm all year round, except 24–26 Dec, 31 Dec, 1 Jan and Easter Sunday |
Tip South Farm, the farmhouse where George Eliot was born, still stands on the Arbury
Estate. Today the estate – owned by the Newdegate family – is often open to the public during
summer bank holidays, with guided tours conducted by the George Eliot Fellowship.

# 6 Basilica Sculpture

*Cov firm's legal case nearly toppled government*

In front of Coventry's Combined Court Centre on Much Park Street is a statue styled to resemble a judge's wig, and reflect the rule of law. Titled *Basilica*, the sculpture was produced by Paul de Menchaux, and unveiled in 1991. Coventry has had its fair share of high-profile legal cases, but none more significant than the Matrix Churchill 'arms-to-Iraq' scandal, which nearly brought down the British Government in the 1990s.

Matrix Churchill was an engineering firm based on Coventry's Fletchamstead highway, that designed and made machine tools. In 1989 it was acquired by Iraqi interests, and began to ship components that could be used to make weapons and parts for missiles to support Saddam Hussein's weapons programme. Following the Gulf War in 1991, focus turned to what degree British firms had supplied Hussein's war effort, and directors from Matrix Churchill were charged with illegal exports. However, during the trial in London documents revealed that British security services had advised on how to export and that a Matrix Churchill executive was an MI6 informant, supplying valuable intelligence on Iraq's arms build-up. The trial collapsed, and Matrix Churchill directors were eventually paid compensation.

An inquiry led to the Arms-to-Iraq report by Sir Richard Scott in 1996. This found that one of the main problems was the government's decision not to tell Parliament of reforms it made to arms export laws to avoid a public outcry. Matrix Churchill had been taken to court for exporting arms without the necessary parliamentary permission, but did have permission under the changed rules.

Sadly, Matrix Churchill collapsed within a couple of years of the arrests, and more than 600 jobs were lost. The scandal damaged the credibility and transparency of John Major's Conservative Government, and in the 1997 general election Tony Blair's Labour Party swept to power.

Address Much Park Street, CV1 2SN | Getting there 12-minute walk from Coventry railway station, 5-minute ride on 12X bus from Pool Meadow station | Hours Unrestricted | Tip Just over the road from the sculpture and courts is the Stone House. This dates from 1350, and only came to light after the Blitz bombings blasted away the brick walls that concealed it.

# 7 Belgrade Theatre

*Coventry's chief centre for culture vultures*

Built in 1958, the Belgrade Theatre was a major part of Coventry's reconstruction following World War II. It was named in recognition of a gift of timber from the Serbian capital city, which was used extensively in the construction. The theatre pioneered the Theatre-in-Education movement in the 1960s, and early company members included theatre luminaries Ian McKellen, Trevor Nunn and Joan Plowright.

The theatre has an 850-seat main auditorium, and is the place to go in the city centre for professional touring productions, from musicals to plays, pantomimes, comedy and live music, plus vibrant community and talent development programmes. It works with young people from disadvantaged backgrounds, using drama as a means to develop personal and social skills, and boost confidence. A smaller secondary studio space, known as B2, holds up to 300. A café and bars line the two-tier foyer, and inside the auditorium there are stalls and a circle, tiers of boxes and a gallery.

Notable performances at the Belgrade included Monty Python's first live performance, in 1971. The Flying Circus TV show had been around a few years, but the Pythons still only had a cult following, so they were delighted to sell out a three-night run at the Belgrade. As Michael Palin recalls in his diaries: 'There were ten men dressed as Gumbies in the front row of the circle.'

In December 2017 the Belgrade was the venue for invited guests and city dignitaries for the announcement of the 2021 UK City of Culture result. Jubilant celebrations featured on national news when Coventry won the bid, seeing off competition from Paisley, Stoke, Sunderland and Swansea. Today, the Belgrade is a Grade II-listed building, with a prominent city crest in pride of place on the auditorium's outer wall. With fountains and seat benches in Belgrade Square, it's a popular place to enjoy the sunshine.

Address Belgrade Square, Corporation Street, CV1 1GS, +44 (0)24 7655 3055, www.belgrade.co.uk | Getting there 14-minute walk from Coventry railway station, 6-minute walk from Pool Meadow bus station | Hours Check website for performances | Tip Check out the Shop Front Theatre, a unique 55-seat space in what was once a fish and chip shop in the City Arcade, now home to independent, award-winning company, Theatre Absolute. In the Shop Front, Theatre Absolute presents new theatre work, commissions writers and artists, runs workshops, and more.

# 8 Berkswell Church

*Pretty Norman church with a chamber of secrets*

St. John the Baptist church in the pretty village of Berkswell lies just outside Coventry's western boundary. It's a beautiful late 12th-century Norman church, part of the diocese of Coventry, and is a Grade I-listed building.

The church contains among the best examples of Norman crypts in the country. Uniquely, it's in two parts, with separate doorways. The crypts are both of a ribbed vault design, with a framework of diagonal arched ribs meeting at a central point. They date back to the 12th century, along with the chancel, nave and north aisle. The western crypt is octagonal, and features a Caen stone font, which dates from the early 19th century. Two archways leading to a south aisle were added during the 14th century, and the castellated tower is believed to have been added around 1600. The tower walls feature a prominent sundial, and also a clock. A rare Sanctus Bell is also on show in the north wall of the nave, which from medieval times would have been rung at the Christian Eucharist, just before bread and wine were consecrated. These bells were banned following the Reformation, and this particular example was discovered hidden high in the church tower, as it underwent restoration in 2011. Another interesting feature of the church is a half-timbered, two-storey south porch, added around 1500. There's also an external stone stairway leading to the upper chamber.

Much of the woodwork inside the church was carved by Robert Thompson between 1926 and 1946. Thompson was known as the Mouseman of Kilburn, and nine of his signature carved mice feature in the woodwork here. The graveyard headstones include that of Maud Watson, who became the first Ladies' Singles Lawn Tennis champion at Wimbledon in 1884, beating her sister in the final. Miss Watson lived with her father, the Rector, at Well House, then the Rectory, which stands next door to the church.

**Address** Church Lane, Berkswell, CV7 7BJ, berkswellchurch.org.uk | **Getting there** Train to Berkswell, then a 30-minute walk | **Hours** Services Sun 8.30am, 10am, 5pm & Thu 10.30am | **Tip** Berkswell takes its village name from the 5-metre-square, stone-walled well next to the churchyard. Once used for baptisms, the coins that lie within are evidence of its continued popularity as a wishing well.

# 9___Big Comfy Bookshop

*Cov's coolest book store and live music venue*

This independent bookshop sits within a renovated former warehouse at the heart of Coventry's creative village, and has doubled in size since it opened. First and foremost, the Big Comfy Bookshop offers thousands of second-hand books, including an eclectic mix of fiction, biography, history, and rare works. But it has also developed and expanded to become more of a bookshop café, and now sells locally produced cakes and craft beers alongside more standard lunchtime fare. The shop's logo says it all – a big, comfy-looking red armchair that conveys the spirit of the Big Comfy Bookshop and its friendly team.

The shop's owner, Michael McEntee, works hard to spread the word via the shop's social media channels, with interesting and regular posts to Facebook, Instagram and Twitter, as well as vlogs on the shop's YouTube channel. 'It's all about local – about supporting creatives and having space to be expressive and be yourself,' says Michael of the shop's ethos, which matches that of the wider FarGo Village.

Music is McEntee's other big passion, and on the first and third Friday of each month the bookshop turns into a venue, with an emphasis on acoustic and folk artists. The bookshop has a reputation for putting on a variety of up-and-coming acts, who enjoy performing in this unique and intimate venue. There are regular, packed-out poetry nights, with performers travelling from far and wide to recite their work to an appreciative and knowledgeable audience, themed nights such as evenings dedicated to retro gaming, as well as writing groups, book clubs, and more.

The Big Comfy Bookshop's recent inclusion in the *Guardian*'s 'Best small UK music venues: readers' travel tips' underlines its growing reputation as one of Coventry's finest, one-of-a-kind venues, offering a relaxed and friendly community hub for the city's creative residents.

Address FarGo Village, Far Gosford Street, CV1 5ED, www.thebigcomfybookshop.co.uk |
Getting there 25-minute walk from Coventry railway station, 8 or 13 bus to Far Gosford
Street | Hours Mon–Sat 11am–4pm | Tip Bookworms shouldn't miss Gosford Books,
another great second-hand bookshop just half a mile away, on Gosford Street: a traditional
second-hand book store that's great for browsing.

# 10  Biggin Hall Pub

*Lovely venue in classic Brewers' Tudor style*

The Biggin Hall Hotel and Public House is a Grade II-listed pub in the Stoke area of Coventry. It's built in the Brewers' Tudor style, a name given to the architectural style applied to pubs constructed in the inter-war years, which it was hoped would conjure up an image of 'merrie England', and attract a new, more respectable middle class customer. The Biggin Hall was one of just 20 pubs across England, among around 5,000 built at this time, that were granted listed status by Historic England in 2015.

While Biggin Hall may not have the rich historical span of some of Coventry's other pubs that stretch back many hundreds of years – such as the Golden Cross (see ch. 92) – it's a fascinating building for a number of reasons. Foremost among these is the fact that it was designed by the prominent, Coventry-based architect Thomas Francis Tickner, who was also responsible for the impressive tribute to the fallen at the centre of Coventry's War Memorial Park (see ch. 108).

Building work began on the Biggin Hall pub in 1921 for the Marston, Thompson and Evershed Brewery – today known simply as Marston's – and was completed and opened in 1923.

The building's exterior features an impressive frontage in a cream-and-black Mock Tudor style, with a steeply pitched roof, half-timbered exterior, tall chimneys and high windows. Chief among the interesting features inside is a cosy, wood-panelled inglenook fireplace. The word 'ingle' is Old English for fire, and an inglenook fireplace has open space and seating on either side of it, for people to sit in the warmth while they chat and enjoy their drinks. The floor plan has carefully separated spaces that reflects the original aim to design the pub as a respectable establishment offering food and drink. The pub was recently refurbished to make the most of its Brewer's Tudor-style design.

Address 214 Binley Road, CV3 1HG, +44 (0)24 7644 2109, www.bigginhallpub.co.uk |
Getting there 13-minute ride on the 13 bus from Pool Meadow station | Hours Daily
midday–11pm | Tip Musicians should visit Express Music, just 50 metres away. Established
in the 1980s, it has around £1-million-worth of stock, including a vast range of guitars.

# 11 Boundary Marker Post

*Blink and miss it London Road landmark*

Now home to around 400,000 people, Coventry has grown considerably since medieval days. Several periods of expansion have occurred over the centuries, and while little remains of early developments, some fascinating signposts remain: the 11th-century monastery built by Leofric, Earl of Mercia, later turned into a priory and cathedral by Bishop Robert de Limesey; Coventry castle, built in the mid-12th-century by the second Earl of Chester, encouraging tradesmen and merchants to settle; churches followed, and the third Earl of Chester stayed in a manor house at Cheylesmore. In 1355, building of the city walls began, with Coventry's footprint then very similar to that of the ring road today. The walls were razed in 1662 after the Civil War, but remains can be found.

Coventry Canal opened in the late 18th century, and the city saw rapid growth of trades such as clothing, clocks, and later, bicycle and car production. In 1842, an Act of Parliament redefined the boundaries, allowing expansion, and by 1890 Coventry encompassed Earlsdon to the west and Radford to the north.

Further expansion in 1928 swallowed up former parishes, and incorporated Tile Hill, Canley and Allesley to the west, Holbrooks and Longford in the north, and as far as Willenhall and Binley to the east. As the city prospered, 1932 saw further eastward growth to Bell Green, Walsgrave and Willenhall. By 1947, the city covered almost 20,000 acres.

The beautiful 1932 boundary marker pictured here is located on London Road, at Toll Barr End, to the south-west of Coventry. It carries the city's crest, and is inscribed with *County of Warwick-Parish of Baginton* on one side, and *City of Coventry* on the other. Several such markers can be found today, indicating boundaries between the city and parishes or former parishes. See how many you can find. But keep a sharp lookout: they're easy to miss!

Address London Road, CV4 4RP | Getting there 30-minute ride on the 21 bus from Pool Meadow station | Hours Unrestricted | Tip Midland Air Museum is just a short walk along Rowley Road. Exhibits include a Vulcan bomber, a MiG, and a Sea Harrier jump jet.

# 12 Boxing Hall of Fame

*Jardine Crescent mural to local ring legends*

Located in Jardine Crescent, the Hall of Fame mural next to Tile Hill Library depicts famous boxing champions with a connection to the Coventry area. Youngsters aged between 11 and 25 from Tile Hill Young People's Centre painted the mural in 2008, and invited the local boxers to attend the unveiling. Some of the sportsmen featured in the painting trained at Tile Hill Social Club, three of whom became British champions.

The boxers in the mural originally included former British heavyweight champion Jack Bodell, who beat Joe Bugner in 1971, and lived in the area for many years. There was the image of Bobby Arthur, British Welterweight champion over 1972–1973, who raised his family in the Tile Hill area, and ran the New Star pub in Jardine Crescent for a number of years – the building being demolished in the early 2000s following a fire. Sadly, the likenesses of Bodell and Arthur have gone. Mick Leahy, also pictured, was born in Ireland and became a British citizen in 1961. He lived the rest of his life in Coventry, and won the British Middleweight title in 1963. At the end of that bout his friend from nearby Leamington, former world boxing champion Randolph Turpin, along with legends Sugar Ray Robinson and Muhammad Ali, jumped into the ring to congratulate him. Leahy even went on to fight and beat Robinson in Scotland in 1964. The mural also includes an image of Muhammad Ali, who drew huge crowds when he famously visited Coventry in 1983 to officially open the Knockout Fish Bar on Jardine Crescent, run by the former British heavyweight champion Jack Bodell. In recent years, the fish bar has been run as an Indian takeaway.

While the mural could perhaps do with a revamp and a fresh coat of paint, it nonetheless remains a vibrant and compelling image to greet people entering Jardine Crescent from Bushbery Avenue, and is well worth a visit for any sporting fan.

**Address** Jardine Crescent, Tile Hill, CV4 9PL | **Getting there** 25-minute ride on the 6 or 6A bus from Pool Meadow to Jardine Crescent in Tile Hill | **Hours** Unrestricted | **Tip** A little over a mile away, the Standard Triumph Recreational Club has been training boxers for decades, with links to Coventry's homegrown European Champion, Errol Christie.

# 13 Caludon Castle Ruins

*Handsome medieval wall in public park*

All that remains of Caludon Castle, on a site dating back to before the Norman Conquest in the 11th century, is a large fragment of sandstone wall. This Grade I- listed relic stands in the middle of Caludon Castle Park, in Coventry's Wyken area.

Once a large house, Caludon was extended into a crenellated castle in the 14th century. It changed hands between noblemen, including Ranulf de Blondeville, Sir John de Segrave – responsible for hunting down the Scottish rebel William Wallace of *Braveheart* movie fame – and Thomas de Mowbray, Duke of Norfolk, who was famous for the aborted Battle of Gosford Green in Coventry, that was touched upon in Shakespeare's play *Richard II*. Mowbray and Henry Bolingbroke, the Duke of Hereford, accused each other of speaking treasonable words against King Richard II. The dispute was to be settled by combat, but the king halted proceedings at the last moment, and banished them both. Bolingbroke later returned and took the throne as Henry IV.

The castle was largely destroyed in 1662, and remained in ruins until 1800, when it was used in the construction of a farmhouse on the site. Originally it was oval in shape and surrounded by a wall with towers. A separate moated site nearly 200 metres to the south of the castle was built in medieval times, and is now a Scheduled Ancient Monument in its own right.

What remains of the castle wall features two large tracery windows, with red sandstone at their edges and also at both ends of the wall. Beneath the large windows are two smaller ones, suggesting an undercroft. The ruins are thought to date from the 14th century. An iron coffin with the remains of a knight in armour was once unearthed during excavation work near the castle. St George and the Dragon-inspired entrance gates to the park acknowledge the local legend that St George, patron saint of England who famously slew a dragon, was born here.

Address Farren Road, Coventry, CV2 5EH | Getting there 20-minute ride on the 8 or 9 bus from Pool Meadow station | Hours Unrestricted | Tip St Mary Magdalene's Church in Wyken Croft, just a 5-minutes' walk away, is a small and attractive Grade I-listed Norman church dating from the 12th century.

# 14 Canal Basin Bouncy Bridge

*Footpath that puts a spring in your step*

The Canal Basin footbridge over Coventry ring road, that carries pedestrians from Bishop Street to Leicester Row, is familiar to locals due to its small – but for some, a little unnerving – bounce. Indeed, walking across it has been likened to being drunk when you're sober!

Pedestrian access to the bridge, close to Junction One of the ring road, is either via long concrete ramp or steps, the latter framed with curved panels. The footbridge is around three metres wide with painted metal handrails for support, and its lower side walls are painted prominently with the words *Canal Basin*. Structurally, there's nothing to worry about, as it was designed by engineers to move up and down a little, allowing for bend and flex. Bridges such as the Canal Basin footbridge have a natural frequency, or number of times that they can move back and forth per second, so when forces such as a number of people crossing the bridge combine with wind disturbance caused by fast-moving high-sided vehicles below, the vibration lines up with this natural frequency and amplifies it. A similar but more significant process caused London's Millennium Bridge to capture national headlines when it swayed alarmingly under the weight of pedestrians at its official opening in 2000. It was crossed by some 90,000 people, with up to 2,000 people at a time, causing a reported sway of up to 70 millimetres. Londoners christened it 'Wobbly Bridge' and it was subsequently closed for modifications and repair work just two days after it was opened. It didn't reopen until 2002.

There were plans to demolish the Canal Basin footbridge around 2015, when it was set to be replaced by a street-level crossing, but strength of local feeling, and some residents' concerns around the safety of a pedestrian crossing at a junction of the ring road, resulted in this plan being shelved.

**Address** St Nicholas Street, CV1 4LY | **Getting there** BS5 or BS7 bus from Pool Meadow station, then a 3-minute walk, or a 20-minute walk from Coventry railway station via Broadgate and the Burges | **Hours** Unrestricted | **Tip** A new Playwrights Café, an offspring of the excellent established bar and bistro of the same name in the Cathedral Quarter on Hay Lane (see ch. 70) opened in the Canal Basin in summer 2020.

# 15 Canal Basin Weigh-bridge

*A glimpse of transport from two centuries ago*

At the entrance to the atmospheric Coventry Basin off Saint Nicholas Street is a weigh-bridge office believed to date from 1810. Built from brick with a slate roof, it served as a toll office, with a cast iron weigh-bridge that weighed vehicles entering and leaving the unusual Y-shaped Coventry Canal Basin. Originally there were two weigh-bridges on either side of the canal, but the one to the north is no longer standing.

The Coventry Canal Company was formed in 1768, and commissioned engineer James Brindley to mastermind the layout of the canal, which would connect with Fradley Junction, around 38 miles to the north, near Lichfield. It was built primarily to transport coal from the pits at Bedworth, Coventry and Nuneaton to the rest of the Midlands and beyond. In its heyday, it was part of the Birmingham – London route via the Birmingham and Fazeley Canal, Coventry Canal, Oxford Canal and River Thames. Today, the canal and its surrounding area from the basin to Hawkesbury Junction is a designated conservation area. Most of the buildings and structures around the basin were built by the Coventry Canal Navigation Company, and are some of the finest surviving examples of such architecture in the West Midlands. Although coal is no longer loaded, the historic warehouses as well as the Canal Bridge and Canal House are all Grade II-listed, and of significant historical interest.

In the early 1990s the city council and British Waterways refurbished and redeveloped the canal basin. Today, the *Coventry Telegraph* is sited here, along with The Tin Music (see ch. 102), while the Warehouse is home to a number of artist studios, but some of the units sit empty. However, with National Lottery Heritage Fund money awarded to the Coventry City of Culture Trust, announced in 2019, with a focus on green spaces, urban sites, waterways and heritage locations, it could be refreshed.

**Address** St Nicholas Street, CV1 4LY | **Getting there** BS5 or BS7 bus from Pool Meadow station, followed by a 3-minute walk, or a 20-minute walk from Coventry railway station via Broadgate and the Burges | **Hours** Unrestricted | **Tip** Famous canal engineer James Brindley was responsible for the initial planning of the canal navigation and continues to look out on to the canal, as a three-quarter life-size sculpture.

# 16 Canal Conservation Trail

*Five-mile art walk through Coventry's north*

Starting at the historic Coventry Canal Basin is an art trail over five miles long, stretching all the way to Hawkesbury Junction. It features 39 high-quality, varied artworks. They were created by 31 artists along with local community artists, who produced seven of the works following workshop sessions with local people.

The canal winds through the northern suburbs of Coventry, and many of the bridges along the way carry markers that map the route of the canal. Most of the old industries that once relied on the canal during the Industrial Revolution and lined its banks – such as Alfred Herberts and Courtaulds – have since been replaced by new development.

The artworks have been in place since the late 1990s, and include some very notable pieces. *The Journeyman* is a bronze sculpture by Stephen Hitchin that illustrates the tools used by the navvies who built the canal, just north of bridge number one at Leicester Row. The Daimler Heritage Marker is a bronze sculpture of a Daimler car by Robert Crutchley, opposite the Daimler Powerhouse. This was home to Britain's first car maker, which produced the first British car in 1897. The Powerhouse is undergoing conversion into a major dedicated space for artists and resident creative companies at the time of writing. The Cable Bridge by Andrew Darke, just a stone's throw from the Daimler sculpture, describes an artistic paint job to the existing cable bridge that crosses the canal next to the former Powerhouse.

Look out for the quirky *Fish Seats* by Kate Turner, produced with children from Eagle Street Play Centre: three, brightly coloured rolled metal and enamel seats in the shape of fish. And be sure to see the *Snake in the Grass*, a collaboration between artists from Arts Exchange produced with local groups – sculptural seating in the form of a huge colour-banded snake, in ceramic mosaic and cement.

Address Begins at the Coventry Canal Basin, St Nicholas Street, CV1 4LY | Getting there BS5 or BS7 bus from Pool Meadow, then a 3-minute walk, or a 20-minute walk from Coventry railway station via Broadgate and the Burges | Hours Always open | Tip There are a few pubs along the way, including the Old Crown in Alderman's Green near the Hawkesbury Junction end of the walk, which serves superb food.

# 17 __ Celebrity Walk of Fame

*Honouring stars who put Coventry on the map*

Set in Priory Place against the backdrop of Holy Trinity Church spire, a water feature that carves out a small oasis of calm at the heart of the city, and opposite the BBC studios, is Coventry's Walk of Fame: 20 bronze plaques celebrating some of the city's sons and daughters, who have excelled on the international stage. Not all were born in Coventry, but each has a strong connection with the city, their inclusion being voted for by Coventrians.

The introduction of this Hollywood-style memorial to the city was the idea of local music historian Pete Chambers, with the first 10 people inaugurated to the Walk of Fame in 2008. The names include Mo Mowlam, who as Northern Ireland Secretary played a key role in the Good Friday Peace Agreement, and Sir Henry Parkes, who was born in Coventry but sailed to Australia in 1839, where he was elected Premier of New South Wales on five occasions, and is remembered as the Father of the Federation. Also among the first 10 names set in bronze were 2-Tone band The Specials, pop impresario Pete Waterman, athlete Dave Moorcroft, who held the 5,000 metres world record for a number of years, and Jimmy Hill, who managed Coventry City Football Club. Medieval legend Lady Godiva was also included, as were inventors Frank Whittle and James Starley – for the jet engine and bicycle, respectively – as was Sir William Lyons, who founded Jaguar Cars.

2009 saw a further 10 stars added following another public vote. This crop included actors Clive Owen, Billie Whitelaw and Sir Nigel Hawthorne, athlete and Olympic gold medallist Marlon Devonish, singers Vince Hill and Hazel O'Connor, pop band The Selecter, industrialist Sir Alfred Herbert, poet Philip Larkin, and the 1987 FA Cup-winning Coventry City football team.

With plenty of benches in the vicinity, the Walk of Fame is a great spot to take a lunchtime break.

**Address** Priory Place, CV1 5SE | **Getting there** Coventry's main bus station, Pool Meadow, is adjacent | **Hours** Unrestricted | **Tip** Just behind Priory Place is the original Blue Coat school, founded in 1714 as a school for girls, close to the ruins of St Mary's Priory and Cathedral. It's an impressive Victorian Gothic-style building, reminiscent of a French chateau.

# 18__Cheylesmore Gatehouse
*Coventry's remarkable register office*

Cheylesmore Gatehouse is all that remains of a fabulous royal manor home that originally had a moat, courtyard, great hall and wings. It was built in the 13th century, believed to be constructed by the Earl of Arundel, and was later owned by Queen Isabella, mother of King Edward III. He in turn gifted the manor and the surrounding Cheylesmore hunting park to his eldest son. He was also named Edward, but was known more widely as the Black Prince, a name believed to have been given to him due to the armour he wore.

The Black Prince proved he was a brilliant military man from the age of just 16, playing a major part in defeating the French army at the Battle of Crecy. In his 20s he led another significant victory against the French at Poitiers, where he took the French king prisoner. When not conducting military campaigns overseas, Edward reportedly spent a lot of time at Cheylesmore Manor.

In 1942, while an engineering firm was knocking down a row of cottages that joined the gatehouse, they made a discovery: when the tiles and ceiling were removed they found a medieval timbered roof underneath, which was actually part of the original medieval hall of Cheylesmore Manor. The demolition work stopped and it was instead listed as an Ancient Monument.

Sadly, despite its status, it was pulled down in 1956 as part of Coventry's wider post-war redevelopment work, leaving just the gatehouse that remains today. Thankfully, this timber building part was dismantled and carefully restored by the council in the 1960s, removing all the render that had previously concealed the timber construction. The building consists of three bays, with the central bay being the original carriageway arch that would have provided access to the manor buildings, and today it operates as Coventry's Register Office, with one of its three restored ceremony rooms called the Black Prince Room.

Address Manor House Drive, CV1 2ND | Getting there 7-minute walk from Coventry railway station | Hours Coventry Register Office Mon–Fri 9.15am–4.30pm; always viewable from the outside | Tip It's just a short walk to Shelton Square to take in the sculpture of Guy of Warwick slaying the Dun Cow.

# 19  Christchurch Spire

*Coventry's most resilient landmark*

Christchurch Spire rises from an octagonal-shaped tower on Coventry's New Union Street, and stands 61 metres (just over 200 feet) tall. It's arguably the most unique and interesting of Coventry's illustrious three spires, thanks to its incredible resilience, twice surviving the destruction of its church to keep its place in Coventry's historic cityscape.

In the early 13th century the Earl of Chester, Ranulf de Blondeville, gave permission to monks of the Franciscan order to build a friary on his Cheylesmore Manor estate, which became known as Greyfriars. It was expanded in the 14th century, taking stone from quarries on the Cheylesmore estate, which had by then passed into the ownership of the crown under Richard II. As such, it became a medium-sized church, measuring some 240 feet by 60 feet – about half the footprint of the first Coventry Cathedral, which still stood at that time (see St Mary's Priory Ruins, ch. 79). The monastic buildings attached to the tower were torn down in 1538 by order of Henry VIII, but the tower and spire were spared, and remained a key element of Coventry's skyline for the following 260 years. The church was rebuilt in the early 19th century, and as there were no more grey friars, it was instead consecrated as Christchurch.

However, the new church lasted little more than 100 years. While it escaped unharmed during the November 1940 Blitz, it was badly damaged in a further air raid the following April. Only the remarkably resilient tower and spire survived.

The base of the tower has had a number of different uses through the centuries. It was reportedly a pigsty for a while following the dissolution of the monasteries, but in more recent years it served as a bar called Inspire, selling specialist imported beers and the production of local artisan breweries, although this closed at the end of 2019.

**Address** New Union Street, CV1 2PS | **Getting there** 8-minute walk from Coventry railway station | **Hours** Unrestricted | **Tip** On Greyfriars Green, just a few minutes' walk from the spire, is a sculpture affectionately known locally as *Trigger*. This 12-foot sculpture of a rearing black horse is formally titled *Bucephalus*, and was created in the 1980s by Coventry's Simon Evans.

# 20 _ Cook Street Gate

*Dramatic remnant of the city's medieval wall*

Cook Street Gate is one of the best-preserved relics of Coventry's medieval past, and the most complete representation of what it would have looked like as a walled city. At the northern tip of Lady Herbert's Garden, a cobbled path runs through the arched gateway – be sure to glance up at the wood panelling as you walk through. There were originally 12 gates as part of the city wall, but Cook Street Gate is one of only two that survive, the second being Swanswell Gate, just 150 metres away at the other end of Lady Herbert's Garden (see ch. 55).

Construction of the city wall and Cook Street Gate began in the early 14th century, the battlement-style crenellations added later that century. Over the centuries Coventry became the best-fortified city in England after London, and withstood days-long sieges during the English Civil War. The wall was pulled down in 1662 on the orders of King Charles II.

Unused for many years, Cook Street Gate has undergone recent repair work, and there is talk of converting the upper room into studio tourist accommodation, effectively making it a mini holiday castle. A grant from the National Lottery Heritage Fund, announced at the end of 2019, was awarded to the Historic Coventry Trust, along with money secured by Coventry City Council to secure capital projects in preparation for Coventry's year as City of Culture in 2021. Both gates are owned by the council, and will be transferred on a long lease to the Trust once it has raised the money for their restoration and reuse. It will be tasked with their preservation for future generations by driving revenue for their long-term maintenance.

There's still a romance about the Cook Street Gate, as it continues to serve its original purpose, recreating the sense of passing through into the inner city that visitors to Coventry would have experienced hundreds of years ago.

**Address** Cook Street, CV1 1RA | **Getting there** Coventry's main central bus station, Pool Meadow, is 200 metres away. | **Hours** Unrestricted | **Tip** Look out for the interesting gargoyle at Swanswell Gate, just 150 metres away.

# 21 Coombe Abbey

*Country house that helped thwart Gunpowder Plot*

A popular day-out destination on the eastern edge of the city, Coombe Abbey Country Park and Hotel is set in 500 acres of parkland, but its genteel setting and appearance belie its fascinating history.

Originally, a Cistercian abbey was founded here in 1150 by Richard de Camville. By 1290, during the reign of Edward I, it had become the richest house in Warwickshire. In 1345, Abbot Geoffrey was murdered here, and it's claimed he still haunts the building today. The abbey was later surrendered to King Henry VIII during the dissolution of the monasteries after his break with the Catholic Church. In 1603, King James I knighted the then owner, Sir John Harington, and left his daughter, Princess Elizabeth, to be educated here, where she'd also be caught up in the infamous Gunpowder Plot.

In 1604, the plotters planned to kill King James and his two sons, and kidnap the princess. A Catholic Regent would be appointed to rule while she remained a minor, and she would marry a Catholic. But when Lord Harington got wind of the plan he sent Elizabeth to the safety of Coventry's walled city, and the plotters were captured or killed.

Coombe was bought by the Craven family in 1622. They later hired Capability Brown for landscaping, and to create the mile-long lake. The property remained in Craven hands until the death of the last Lord Craven in 1921, after which it was sold to John Gray. It was bought in 1964 by the council, which opened 150 acres as a country park. It restored the house with a hotel group, and it was reopened as a hotel in the 1990s. The council bought back the hotel in 2017 for £11 million.

Along with woodlands, formal gardens, and an arboretum around the Serpentine lake, there's also a café, gift shop, as well as ceramic and woodturning workshops. More recently a Go Ape aerial treetop course and climbing forest were added to entertain visiting families.

Address Brinklow Road, Binley, CV3 2AB, +44 (0)24 7645 3720, www.coventry.gov.uk/ coombe | Getting there 25-minute ride on 585 bus from Pool Meadow station | Hours Country Park daily 5am–9pm | Tip The park contains a sculpture trail by artist John Wakefield, the most notable being a carving of a Cistercian monk from a giant redwood.

# 22 Coventry God Cakes

*Local delicacy for those with a sweet tooth*

When it comes to local delicacies that are unique to the city, first on the menu has to be the Coventry God Cake. This is even though these sweet treats aren't widely available from the city's bakeries, and many Coventrians have never even heard of them!

Coventry God Cake is a dessert item consisting of sweet mincemeat wrapped in a deliciously crisp baked puff pastry, brushed with milk. Dating back some 700 years, it's understood that God Cakes were made by godparents to give to godchildren with blessings for the coming year, as a New Year tradition in Coventry. These pastry delights taste similar to a regular Christmas mince pie, but crucially, God Cake is produced in a triangular shape, with finishing touches being three slits and a sprinkling of sugar on top of the pastry. The three-sided shape and three slits are said to signify the Holy Trinity, although some argue that they reflect the city's three spires. Some bakers like to jazz God Cakes up even more, with a sweet filling made from currants, orange peel, other spices, or even a drop of rum.

God Cake survived over the centuries thanks to a number of Coventry bakers keeping the tradition alive, but they have fallen out of circulation in recent years, which is why some locals haven't heard of them. In 2012, however, armed with an old God Cake recipe from celebrated local historian David McGrory, Leigh Waite baked her first batch of the treats for that year's annual Heritage Weekend. They proved such a success that she launched her own local business, baking God Cakes for select establishments, including Esquires Coffee House in the city. While the Heritage Cake Company is taking a break from baking for the foreseeable future, the good news is that the Belgrade Theatre's own in-house café also bakes the sweet treats on site, so why not take in a show, and enjoy a bit of Coventry's baking history?

Address Belgrade Café Bar, Belgrade Square, Corporation Street, CV1 1GS, +44 (0)24 7655 3055, www.belgrade.co.uk | Getting there 14-minute walk from Coventry railway station, or 6-minute walk from Pool Meadow bus station | Hours Mon–Sat 10am–11pm | Tip An 8-minute walk away, on New Union Street is Kahawa Café, a popular, family-run, independent specialist coffee shop.

# 23_ Coventry Market

*Like a spaceship that sells everything!*

Coventry has had a vibrant market in the same location since 1958. It's housed in a circular building that looks like a science fiction spaceship, with indoor stalls and kiosks, some of which were established as far back as the 1960s. These traditional outlets offer a huge variety of products. There's a record shop, candy emporium, deli counter, baker, fruit and vegetable kiosks, butcher and fishmonger, perfume and cosmetics stalls, gifts, halal meat, flowers, shoe repairs, key cutting and engraving, clothing and carpets, and much more. You can even get a massage!

Part of the market's charm is its circular design. At its centre is a mini, old-fashioned merry-go-round, the Coventry Market Roundabout, which has been a siren call for children down the generations. There's an old-fashioned bus, Wells Fargo coach and river steamboat. Seats line this area for weary parents to take a break from their shopping to watch the kids. Overhead is a central circular roof light, and even the floor is interesting, with its mosaic design featuring a sun motif in the middle.

This Grade II-listed building was designed in 1957 by Coventry City Architects' Department, and opened by Princess Alexandra the following year. Inside, tall V-shaped concrete columns support the roof and its car park, while the market stalls are of traditional timber construction. Above the market office is a mural by art students from Dresden. Commissioned for the market in a 1950s' Socialist Realist style, this depicts people at work in farming and industrial settings. Some of the supports feature interesting figures such as sailors, mermaids and Neptune.

In its heyday, the market was bustling, but competition from supermarkets and declining numbers of city centre visitors have taken their toll. Nevertheless, Coventry market remains a fascinating place to visit, especially if you're looking for an unusual gift.

Address Market Way, CV1 1DL, +44 (0)24 7622 4927, coventrymarket@coventry.gov.uk |
Getting there 10-minute walk from Coventry railway station | Hours Mon–Wed, Fri & Sat
8.30am–5pm, Thu 8.30am–2.30pm | Tip A 5-minute walk west of the market, past the old
Ikea building and through the underpass beneath the ring road will bring you to Vignoles
Bridge, on Meadow Street in Spon End. This is a cast-iron, single-span footbridge over the
River Sherbourne, designed by Charles Vignoles and built around 1835.

# 24_ Coventry Music Museum
*Tribute to the city's homegrown hit-makers*

Located at the heart of Coventry's 2-Tone Village (see ch. 1), Coventry Music Museum deserves an entry of its own in this edition of *111 Places...*, as while half of the museum's focus is on the late 1970s' music movement, the rest is a celebration of other great Coventry musicians and performers, and those from the surrounding areas of Rugby, Leamington Spa, Nuneaton and Bedworth.

In 2018, this independently-run, small but packed museum was ranked as the best museum in the West Midlands by reviewers on Tripadvisor, coming ahead of big hitters such as the Black Country Living Museum, and Bournville's Cadbury World. Founded by Coventry art historian Pete Chambers and his wife Julie, the Music Museum is manned entirely by volunteers. It has a permanent display dedicated to pioneer in electronic music Delia Derbyshire, who created the Doctor Who theme tune (see ch. 28), Coventry bands King – most famous for their hit *Love and Pride* – The Enemy, The Specials, The Primitives, Hazel O'Connor and Frank Ifield. Coventry's entire music heritage is here, ranging from music hall, rock 'n' roll, the 1960s scene, and even a recreation of the John Lennon and Yoko Ono Bench, a tribute to the 'Acorns for Peace' scandal (see ch. 84).

Among the painstakingly collected and lovingly curated exhibits and permanent fixtures are lots of fun and interactive exhibits, such as a studio where visitors can try composing and making their own music. You can even get your photograph taken in the 1961 Vauxhall Cresta car that featured in the music video that supported The Specials' UK number one hit, *Ghost Town*. There's also the organ Jerry Dammers used to write and record the track. The passionate team of volunteers at Coventry Music Museum has a wealth of knowledge about the city and its music, with a level of enthusiasm that's utterly infectious.

Address 74–80 Walsgrave Road, CV2 4ED, +44 (0)7971 171441, www.covmm.co.uk |
Getting there 7-minute ride on the 9 bus from Pool Meadow station | Hours Thu–Sat
10am–4pm, Sun 10am–3pm | Tip Just a 5-minute walk south is a blue plaque for Siegfried
Bettmann, fixed to the wall of his former home in North Avenue, Stoke. Bettmann was the
founder of Triumph Motorcycles in Coventry, and once a city mayor.

# 25  Coventry Ring Road

*Dual carriageway loop like a roller coaster ride*

The opening sequence to the hit movie *Spooks* (2015) was filmed in an underpass section of Coventry's elevated ring road, which loops round the city centre. In the movie, a convoy transporting a terrorist is attacked by motorcyclists, and an adrenaline-fuelled sequence follows. Junction two of the ring road near Hillfields stands in for London's M4 motorway in the movie, but at one point two of Coventry's three spires are clearly visible.

Coventry ring road, also known as the A4053, is a dual carriageway which forms a 3.6-kilometre loop around the city centre. It was part of Sir Donald Gibson's grand vision for the pedestrianised city centre. The first section was completed in 1959, and the final section not completed until 1974.

The ring road has nine junctions, many of which are grade separated – that is, where inbound roads to the city centre meet the ring road loop, the two roads are at different heights. As a result, the ring road has a mix of several elevated sections and underpasses. Visitors often find the ring road difficult to negotiate – the distance between junctions is rather short in some cases, and given that traffic joining the ring road has to filter with traffic exiting it at speed, it can cause a good deal of consternation. It's also 'back-to-front' for large stretches, in that drivers need to keep in the right-hand lane of the dual carriageway, normally the overtaking lane, to stay on. The ring road's speed limit is 40 miles per hour, and traffic enters and exits at close to this speed, sharing the same slip road, often giving limited distance to weave.

Locals tend to either love it or hate it, with fans and critics likening it to a Scalextric set or a roller-coaster ride. For a couple of days each June, it becomes a sprint circuit as part of the Coventry MotoFest event, which is a popular cultural celebration of motoring madness.

**Address** Coventry, CV1 | **Getting there** Sections of the ring road pass alongside Coventry railway station and Pool Meadow bus station | **Hours** Always open | **Tip** Coventry's Cathedral Quarter is a 7-minute walk away and starred in the Nativity movies, written and directed by West Midlands native Debbie Isitt, which featured Catherine Tate and David Tennant.

# 26___Coventry Watch Museum

*Journey back in time at this industrial shrine*

Housed in 19th-century cottages, with a Victorian-style toilet block and a World War II air raid shelter, Coventry Watch Museum is a wonderful gem that transports visitors back in time, telling the story of an industry that was central to the city's historical development.

Coventry's earliest recorded watchmaker was Samuel Watson, who was active in the city in the late 17th century, and made two astronomical clocks incorporating planetary motion for King Charles II. The second of these still survives today, and is part of the Queen's collection in Windsor Castle. Throughout the 18th and 19th centuries, Coventry was one of the main watchmaking centres in the country, and by 1860 there were around 90 separate manufacturers located in the city. However, competition from cheaper manufacturing techniques in America, and high-quality watchmaking in Switzerland, took their toll, and watchmaking began to die out in Coventry. However, the city's skill base for precision engineering would continue to be applied in the bicycle and car-making industries.

The Coventry Watch Museum Project was established in 1995, and in 2002 it bought premises on medieval Spon Street. The Museum is set up using the ground floor of the existing buildings, tucked away down the side and to the back of the Samoan Joes Tiki cocktail bar. The museum is open on Tuesday and Saturday each week, and visitors get to see exhibitions of Coventry-made clocks, watches and tooling, plus other artefacts and family history records – all fascinating details of the city's once-thriving watchmaking heritage, and insight into how people lived and worked two centuries ago. Today it's manned by enthusiastic volunteers, with famous visitors down the years including Michael Portillo, who visited the museum for his *Great Railway Journeys* series. There's also an interesting World War II display.

Address Spon Street, CV1 3BA, +44 (0)7973 627200, www.coventrywatchmuseum.co.uk |
Getting there 13-minute walk from Coventry railway station along Starley Road and Croft
Road | Hours Tue & Sat 11am–3pm | Tip Check out the spectacular crack in the exterior
wall of the cottages that house the Coventry Watch Museum, caused by WW2 bombing.

# 27 Dashing Blades Barbers

*The coolest haircut and beard trim in town*

It's clear from the retro, vintage-style typeface and ornate detailing on the signage and opening hours that adorn the Dashing Blades windows and store front, that this is a retro-style traditional venue. Walk through the doors into the inner sanctum, and you're met with the vibe of a traditional gentlemen's club.

The owner, Rob Walton, gave up a career as a teacher to follow his passion. With his round spectacles, voluminous beard and long hair, it's clear he has a keen personal interest in male grooming. You'll usually find him dressed in a stylish three-piece suit, set off by two-tone brogues. Serious and quietly spoken, you can imagine how bemused he would have been when he was included in the 'Hot List' of 40 of the best-looking people in Coventry and Warwickshire as published by local newspaper the *Coventry Telegraph* in 2017. The Dashing Blades barbershop owner is described in the article as 'nothing short of dashing himself'.

Rob first opened a barber shop in FarGo Village as a one-man operation in 2014, but has since moved and expanded premises within the village, and taken on more staff. As well as haircuts, Dashing Blades also offers beard styling and trimming, plus hot towel cut-throat shaves. As a result the clientele isn't limited to the city's huge student population and Coventrians, but committed beard growers are prepared to travel from far and wide to partake of the venue's services and make a day out of it in the FarGo Village.

Blues and jazz music plays in the background, and a set of wall-mounted antlers take pride of place on the wall. There's a comfy button-back leather sofa, Persian rug, vintage wooden furniture, eye-catching framed artwork – including a painting of Walton himself by one of his customers – and large ornately framed mirrors. It's the kind of environment in which a gentleman can sit back, relax, and be pampered.

**Address** FarGo Village, Far Gosford Street, CV1 5ED, +44 (0)24 7693 5677, www.dashingbladesbarbershop.resurva.com | **Getting there** 25-minute walk from Coventry railway station; bus 8 or 13 to Far Gosford Street from Pool Meadow station | **Hours** Mon–Sat 10am, closing time varies from 4–6pm | **Tip** A 5-minute walk back into town brings you to the Lanchester Library. This is nicknamed 'the castle' due to its turrets, which are reminiscent of a prison, but in reality it represents a fine example of thoughtful architecture that prioritises sustainable energy use and natural ventilation.

# 28 Delia Derbyshire

*Homage to Coventry-born sculptress of sound*

There is a life-sized portrait of Delia Derbyshire – the electronic music pioneer famous for creating the Doctor Who theme tune – along with a plaque, spray-painted by artist Stewy onto a Coventry University building for International Women's Day in 2018. Derbyshire was born in Coundon in Coventry in 1937. Growing up in the city during the Blitz, she said in later life that the air raid sirens she'd heard as a child influenced her music.

As a girl, Derbyshire was a gifted musician, playing violin and piano to a high standard. She won a scholarship to study at Cambridge University, where she began to experiment with abstract sounds in compositions. She later became a teacher, and tried to break into the male-dominated record industry. She finally joined the BBC as a trainee assistant studio manager, and landed a job at the BBC's Radiophonic Workshop in 1962, where she worked for 11 years. It was here that the BBC created experimental soundtracks, often with a sci-fi flavour. Derbyshire made use of everyday objects to create music for radio and TV programmes, and it was during this time that she recorded the iconic Doctor Who theme tune. Although the music was written by Ron Grainer, the finished product was unrecognisable – Grainer would later acknowledge that she had changed his original work so much that the writer credit should at least be shared.

Derbyshire also worked outside the BBC with various collaborators to create and promote electronic music, and has been cited as an influence on bands including the Chemical Brothers, Pink Floyd and Orbital. There's a display, including her tape recorders, on show at the Coventry Music Museum.

Derbyshire died in 2001, aged just 64. A blue plaque was unveiled in 2017 at 104 Cedars Avenue, where she lived in Coventry, and a street – Derbyshire Way – was named after the composer.

Address 34–35 Jordan Well, CV1 5RW | Getting there 6-minute walk from Pool Meadow bus station, 15-minute walk from Coventry railway station | Hours Unrestricted | Tip It's a 5-minute walk to the open space in Little Park Street where the benches incorporate sculpted horses. This is the work of Jim Brown, who worked in the Coventry City Architects' Department in the post-war years.

# 29 Devil's Dungeon

*BMX biking for kids through the decades*

The Kenilworth Road woodlands run alongside this main route from Coventry's city centre. There were originally three rows of oak trees, planted in the 18th century, to ensure an impressive approach to Coventry from the south. These oaks have been joined over the years by lime trees, beech, silver birch, sycamore, rowan and poplars. The woodlands along the route are now part of a conservation area, established in the 1960s. In the Stivichall Common section of the woodlands, near to an intriguing garden wall made of old gravestones, on the corner where Beechwood Avenue and Kenilworth Road meet, is a contoured depression that has been the playground of Coventry's BMX biking enthusiasts for decades. This area is known locally as Devil's Dungeon.

Some locals claim that Devil's Dungeon is a crater that was caused by a bomb dropped by a Zeppelin, but records show that the only Zeppelin to successfully target Coventry during World War I dropped its bombs on the Baginton Sewage Works, and in the grounds of Whitley Abbey, out to the east of the city. The depression is more likely the remains of a stone pit, where stone was once quarried and extracted for building and for other purposes, but it's also thought that the pit was dug deeper by Royal Munster Fusilier solders. These soldiers were stationed in Coventry for a spell in 1915, and were reportedly testing a new tool that would be used for digging the trenches that were so integral to the fighting in the First World War.

Down the years the deep depression has been shaped and re-shaped into a succession of ramps, hollows and jumps by teenage bikers keen to develop their BMX skills, and by remote-controlled car enthusiasts. Kids from all over Coventry visit Devil's Dungeon, and for non-cyclists it's easy to spend an hour or two watching BMXers of various skill levels tackle the course with enthusiasm.

Address Corner of Beechwood Avenue and Kenilworth Road, CV3 6BB | Getting there 15-minute ride on the 12X bus from Pool Meadow station | Hours Always open | Tip A little over half a mile away is Earlsdon Street, with a good selection of independent coffee shops such as Sage, Bravo and Emily's.

# 30___Dhillon's Brewery

*Home to craft beers with a hint of madness*

Approaching Dhillon's Brewery, you pass the Ricoh arena, home to Wasps rugby club and the former stadium of Coventry City's Sky Blues football club, into an industrial estate. You might think you're in the wrong place as you pass expensive-looking motor repairs, until you spot the funky artwork and sheltered beer garden of Dhillon's Brewery.

Dhillon's is a real ale micro-brewery, where they like to 'Keep it Re'ale' by producing craft beers with – according to its website – a 'hint of madness'. Conceived in 2015, it takes its name from founder Dal Dhillon, whose family emblem, the lion, is the basis of the brand logo. The factory unit contains both the brewing operation and storage facilities, a tap room, a pool table or two, and speakers for music. It's a very cool, warehouse-chic set up, but with a zany homeliness and sense of style, such as artwork by local artists.

A big part of the brewery's ethos is that it feels like a community hub, producing superb beers with a local hook. It also hosts local bands and stand-up comedy events, and has support from other local businesses, such as the local wrestling team. There are beer tours with master brewer Pedro, who will show off the fermenting vessels, mash tuns and shiny brewing kit. There's even a new gin still on site.

The brewery has four core beers: Bright Eyes golden pale ale, Amber Gambler, Fair Lady hazy pale ale, and Red Rebel, a strong ruby red IPA. Lager offerings include Allegre Steam lager, and Sky Blue Army lager – the official beer of the football club. Seasonal beers are also brewed here, and sold in local venues as well as online. But perhaps the coolest canned drink of all is Ghost Town lager, a German-style pilsner presented in a funky black and white can, and which represents a nod to the 2-Tone music for which the city is famous, its name a tribute to the 1981 hit song by The Specials.

**Address** Unit 14a, Hales Industrial Estate, Rowley's Green Lane, Longford, CV6 6AT, +44 (0)24 7666 7413, www.dhillonsbrewery.com | Getting there 10-minute walk from Coventry Arena railway station, 25-minute ride on the 3 bus from Pool Meadow station | Hours Fri 5–10pm, Sat 4–10pm, check website for brewery tours | Tip For an alternative night out, and if you're feeling flush, the Grosvenor Casino in the Ricoh Arena complex is open until 6am Mon–Thu, and 24 hours Fri–Sun.

# 31_Elephant Sports Centre

*This jumbo facility is a modernist masterpiece*

The Coventry Sports and Leisure Centre was a building of two distinct halves: the first was the Olympic swimming pool, with its high diving boards and kids' pool with fun slides, which was built in 1966; the second, connected by a long walkway, was the quirky, industrialist sports centre built in 1976, which housed gyms, squash courts, and other leisure facilities.

The swimming pool, with its three-storey glass wall and W-shaped roofline looks out onto Coventry University – formerly Lanchester Polytechnic – with glimpses of Coventry's new and old cathedral behind, and is Grade II-listed. However, the sports centre – or 'the Elephant' as it's known to locals – is not a listed building.

Despite its lack of architectural acknowledgement, the Elephant is undoubtedly one of Coventry's most distinctive landmarks. Whether visiting on foot or passing through in a car on the elevated ring road, almost within touching distance of the building's strange grey, zinc-panelled shell, the Elephant is an arresting sight at any time of day.

Designed by Terence Gregory and Harry Noble of the City Architects department of the time, the building cost around £750,000 to build. It is perched atop massive tapered concrete pillars and is a modernist take on the city's coat of arms, which features an elephant holding up a castle at its centre and is perhaps the single most recognisable symbol of Coventry. Triangles of glass and peaked hoods of zinc panels break the grey shell to represent an elephant's eyes, tusks and ears, all with a modernist flavour.

Sadly the unprofitable sports and leisure centre was closed in late 2019, after a large ultra-modern swimming pool and water park complex – the Wave – was constructed as a replacement. There are rumours that the mothballed site is set to become a new cultural hub, but the Elephant's true fate has yet to be revealed.

Address Fairfax Street, CV1 5RY | Getting there Coventry's main bus station, Pool Meadow, is 100 metres away | Hours Unrestricted | Tip Walk underneath the belly of the Elephant Sports Centre up Cox Street, turn right, and within 5 minutes you'll arrive at The Herbert gallery. The crest of Coventry's Coat of Arms, carved by sculptor John Poole, features an elephant, and is located high on the gallery's end wall.

# 32 Ellen Terry Building

*One of the first female stage superstars*

Coventry-born Dame Alice Ellen Terry was a great female actor, and one of the first female stars of the stage. Terry took the acting world by storm at the turn of the 20th century, achieving huge popularity with Victorian audiences. Today her name graces the Ellen Terry Building, previously the Gaumont Palace Theatre and later Odeon cinema. Today it's a Grade II-listed building, and part of Coventry University.

Terry was born in Coventry in 1847 to a family of actors – indeed her sister, Kate, was grandmother of the actor Sir John Gielgud. Ellen was a child actor, first appearing in Shakespeare plays in London at the age of nine, and touring throughout Britain in her teens. In 1878 she joined the Henry Irving company as his leading lady, and for more than 20 years was acknowledged as the finest Shakespearean and comic actress in Britain. The company even toured America. Terry changed direction in 1903, becoming manager of London's Imperial Theatre and producing plays by George Bernard Shaw and Henrik Ibsen. She continued to act on stage until 1920, and in the early years of films from 1916 to 1922. Terry also gained notoriety for her personal life. She first married at the age of 16 to an artist 30 years her senior, although this lasted less than a year. She subsequently had three further marriages, two illegitimate children, and several romantic liaisons that reads like a who's who of stars of the day.

The iconic building was named after Terry in commemoration of the golden age of cinema. The building was refurbished in 2000, updated with a more modern appearance while maintaining its art deco heritage. Inside there's a ballroom, a stage for concerts, a proscenium arch, and an organ rising from the floor of the orchestra. Visitors can avail themselves of the restaurant above the art deco foyer. Coventry university holds an archive of Terry memorabilia.

Address 34-35 Jordan Well, CV1 5RW | Getting there 6-minute walk from Pool Meadow bus station, 15-minute walk from Coventry railway station | Hours Always viewable from the outside | Tip Next to the Ellen Terry building is the Phoenix pub, a marvellous listed house with art nouveau gables, built in 1906. The Phoenix is always lively and serves great food.

# 33 Esquires Coffee House
*Relax in an oasis of calm at the heart of the city*

Esquires Coffee House is attached to Coventry Transport Museum on Hales Street, at the corner of Millennium Place. Opened in 2008, it's a franchise of the international coffee house chain founded in Canada, and which has opened some 50 stores in the UK, and more than 10 in Ireland, since 2000.

Esquires serves organic Fair-trade coffee and food, and doesn't have the fast-food quality of some larger UK chains. The breakfast and brunch menus are varied, and al fresco seating overlooks the Whittle Arch, Public Bench and Glass Bridge of Millennium Place. Sitting inside offers good views of Coventrians going about their business at one of the city's busier intersections, through the full-height, glass panelled store front. Seating is a mix of fabric tub chairs, wood and metal chairs, with tables of varying sizes. The wall decorations and framed artwork pay tribute to Coventry's history of car and cycle manufacturing, and the joy of travel. Popular choices on the in-store breakfast and brunch menu include smashed avocado on toast, eggs benedict, and a full vegan breakfast. Shakes and smoothies, cold presses and fresh juices complement the range of teas and coffees on offer, the latter decorated with latte art or some other barista flourish. At lunch time there are soups, sandwiches or baguettes and jacket potatoes to choose from.

Esquires also offers external catering and delivers food boxes to local addresses, which received rave reviews throughout 2020. The line-up includes boxed afternoon tea with a bottle of Prosecco, breakfasts or lunches, scones, cookies or pastries.

The franchisee runs the establishment with the flair and creativity of an independent shop. Activities have included raising money for charity on long-distance cycling events, launching an apprentice scheme, and arranging smoothie classes with local schoolchildren, making this branch of Esquires a real Coventry community hub.

**Address** Transport Museum, Millennium Place, CV1 1JD, +44 (0)24 7625 7300, www.esquirescoffeecoventry.co.uk | Getting there Coventry's main bus station, Pool Meadow, is adjacent | Hours Mon–Fri 9am–3pm, Sat 10am–3pm | Tip Castle Yard Tap Room, just off Hay Lane, is a 5-minute walk away, in a stunning location next to the Guildhall, and offers a good selection of beers.

# 34 Finney's Coffee Co

*Cool place to grab a cup o' Joe*

Finney's Coffee Co has built a reputation as one of the coolest and most stylish independent coffee shops in Coventry since it opened in 2016. It's located on Warwick Row, where many of the white-painted and red-brick Victorian townhouses are listed, and occupied by high-end businesses such as solicitors and premium estate agents. It's also within yards of the eye-catching James Starley statue (see ch. 49).

The first thing you notice about Finney's is its distinctive exterior styling. The Finney's Coffee Co logo is picked out against black signage above the doors and on the black awnings out front. The outdoor seating area is contained by black café barriers, also featuring the Finney's logo, often with tall potted bamboo plants, plus rattan-style seats and wood-topped tables. The café has vertical wood panelling to its frontage with large glass windows on either side of the doors. High stools and a bar-style bench allow customers to sit side-by-side, looking out onto pretty Greyfriars Green, with its lovingly manicured floral gardens. Inside, dozens of warm, tungsten-style exposed-bulb lights in various shapes and sizes hang from the ceiling, while a convex glass counter displays a selection of mouth-watering cakes and pastries. A number of small, square wooden tables are surrounded with seats, and there are several breakfast bar-style tables.

And as well as the cool and relaxed ambience, there's the coffee itself: Finney's serves Union coffee, a brand with a reputation for the quality of its roasting, but also for its ethically-sourced beans. On the food front, the shop menu includes well-presented toasties and bagels. With free WiFi, USB charging ports and plenty of electricity sockets available, it's the ideal place to kick back with a coffee and catch up on the latest posts, or finalise that perfect guide book entry.

**Address** 25 Warwick Row, CV1 1EY, +44 (0)24 7655 4440 | **Getting there** 6-minute walk from Coventry railway station through pretty Greyfriars Green | **Hours** Mon–Fri 9am–5.30pm, Sat 9am–6pm, Sun 10am–5pm | **Tip** Bean and Leaf is another great independent coffee shop just a 5-minute walk away. Coffee in this family-run shop, who describe themselves as coffee geeks and bakers, is from Caravan Coffee Roasters.

# 35 Foleshill Road

*Showcasing world fashion, food and heritage*

Foleshill is a residential, industrial and commercial area north-east of Coventry's city centre, running through which is the aptly-named Foleshill Road. With the Coventry Canal and a railway in the area, it became an industrial hub during Victorian times. It was home to ribbon weaving factories such as J&J Cash, Courtaulds Ltd, which was a world leader in producing artificial fibres, plus car plants Jaguar and Riley Cars, and cycle maker Challenge. For a number of years it was also home to the writer George Eliot (see ch. 40). Legendary old pub the General Wolfe, which began its life as a tavern in the early 19th century, was once an iconic music venue. While today it's a restaurant, in its music venue heyday of the 1970s and 1980s, the Wolfe hosted big-name bands such as U2 and the Eurythmics.

Following World War II, the area saw a major influx of Commonwealth migrants, drawn to the availability of industrial and manufacturing work. The 1960s saw many arrivals from South Asia – predominantly India – as well as those of African-Caribbean origin. Many of these communities made Foleshill their home, and today it's a haven of multiculturalism, welcoming refugees and asylum-seekers, plus migrants from the European Union. It's also the home to many recent arrivals who have escaped persecution in their home countries, and from conflict-torn regions.

Ethnic diversity is widely celebrated in Coventry, and the city is well known for its eclectic mix of cultures. This is showcased along the Foleshill Road, which is lined with a colourful mix of shops and eateries, often with their own ethnic specialisms. The ribbon weaving and manufacturing of the past has been replaced by restaurants of all types, dedicated grocery stores with stalls of colourful and exotic fruit and vegetables, high-end jewellery shops, and outlets offering colourful saris and other couture.

Address Foleshill Road, CV6 5JW | Getting there Short ride on the 20 bus from Pool Meadow station | Hours Always open | Tip If you've got a sweet tooth, be sure to invest in just-made Indian sweets from Standard Sweet Centre and Panjab Sweet Centre at the top of Foleshill Road. They're hugely popular during festivals such as Diwali and Eid.

# 36 Ford's Hospital

*Historic almshouse that's a hit with Dr Who fans*

Also known as Greyfriars Hospital, Ford's Hospital is a timbered almshouse. It's a lovingly restored 16th-century building that's considered one of the finest examples of architecture from that period in the UK today. The Grade I-listed building was founded in 1509 as an almshouse for five men by William Ford, a Coventry wool merchant and former Coventry Mayor. It was enlarged by the executor of Ford's will, William Pisford, and by the 18th century had become a home exclusively for 15 elderly women, as reflected in its signage: *Fords Hospital – Alms house for old ladies of Coventry.*

The building took a direct hit during the Blitz of 14 October, 1940, which saw the matron, her assistant and six residents killed. Unlike a number of other timbered buildings in Coventry, which were relocated to Spon Street (see ch. 61), Ford's Hospital remained as a ruin until 1953, when it was restored on its original site, and to its original design, and reopened by Sir Alfred Herbert. In recent years it was given another makeover, and turned into flats, but still offers sheltered, retirement and supported housing for older Coventrians. Its gated garden features an ornamental fountain, heather and shrubs, that are subject to careful topiary.

The timber-framed architecture sees the first floor jettied out onto the street, with three gables with windows above extending even further. At the middle of the ground floor there's a gate, where it's possible to see that the building encloses a courtyard nearly 4 metres wide and 12 metres long, above which the upper floor also jetties over.

In 2006, the building was used as a location to film an episode of Doctor Who called *The Shakespeare Code*, in which the Doctor, played by David Tennant, goes back in time to meet William Shakespeare and thwart a plot by witches to manipulate one of his plays and free them from imprisonment.

Address Greyfriars Lane, CV1 2GY | Getting there 10-minute walk from Coventry railway station | Hours Always viewable from the outside | Tip Less than half a mile to the south-east, just outside the ring road, is the remarkable Whitefriars Monastery, and what remains of a 14th-century Carmelite friary.

# 37 Francis Skidmore Plaque
*Memorial to a great metal craftsman*

Francis Skidmore, born in 1817, was raised, lived and worked in Coventry and widely lauded as the greatest metal craftsman of the Victorian age. A memorial plaque on the wall of Coventry University's Alma Building, on Alma Street in the Hillfields area of the city, marks the site of his foundry.

As an apprentice to his father – also Francis, and himself a watchmaker, jeweller and silversmith – Skidmore studied architecture and metalwork, and learned how to mount stones, engrave and enamel, and together they founded Francis Skidmore & Son in 1845. Among the earliest known examples of Skidmore's work was a chalice made for St John the Baptist Church in Coventry, but his work really came into its own in the 1850s. At the Great Exhibition of 1851 he displayed a silver gilt and enamelled chalice, made using an innovative new technique called electroplating, which deposited a thin layer of silver onto another metal. It's a work that can still be seen today at London's Victoria and Albert Museum.

Skidmore's chief interest lay in making large-scale metalwork, often in the Gothic revivalist style, and he began to produce for others, such as the architect Sir George Gilbert Scott. It was with Scott that Skidmore worked on the Lichfield, Hereford and Salisbury Cathedral choir screens, and also the Albert Memorial in London. The Hereford screen was hailed as a masterpiece at the 1862 International Exhibition in London. At over 30 feet wide and 30 feet high, its intricacy showcased the skills he had developed as a jewellery maker. This piece can also be seen at the V&A.

During his lifetime Skidmore created works for 24 cathedrals and more than 300 parish churches, including a pulpit in St Michael's Church, the old cathedral in Coventry, which was destroyed in the Blitz. Sadly, however, Skidmore spent his final years in poverty, living on Coventry's Eagle Street, with failing eyesight.

Address Alma Building, Alma Street, CV1 5QA | Getting there 6-minute walk from Pool Meadow bus station | Hours Unrestricted | Tip A 5-minute walk away on Paynes Lane is Coventry Stoves and Fireplaces, formerly the Binley Oak pub, which was the prime rehearsal place for Coventry 2-Tone bands The Specials and The Selecter.

# 38  Frank Whittle Statue

*Jet pioneer and unsung British inventor*

On 12 April, 1937, when the turbine began to spin on the proto-type jet engine developed by Coventry-born engineer Frank Whittle, military aviation changed forever, and the gears of air travel for the masses were set in motion. Today, a statue of Sir Frank Whittle stands in Coventry's Millennium Place, beneath the impressive symmetrical swoops of the Whittle Arch. The statue shows him at RAF Cran-well, watching the first test flight of a jet-propelled Gloster-Whittle E28/39, Britain's first jet aircraft. But many fans feel his achievements still don't receive the true recognition they deserve.

Born in Coventry in 1907, Whittle failed a series of RAF medi-cals in his youth – first because he was too short and too thin – but by 1929 he was a pilot officer in the RAF. While he loved flying, he was no fan of the noise made by the propeller aircraft he flew, and so started the quest that led to his patenting a design for the jet engine in 1930.

Whittle's father, Moses, worked for the Coventry tool-making giant Alfred Herbert Ltd, so from childhood Frank had an under-standing of engineering and metals, which fed into his later inven-tion. After the UK's Air Ministry dismissed Whittle's blueprint in 1929, he co-founded Power Jets Ltd in 1936, and by 1940 the Air Ministry had placed its first order for a jet engine.

Intriguingly, Whittle shunned the wealth that should have fol-lowed the development of that first jet-powered British plane. When the government took over the business in 1944 he wouldn't take the money for his shares, firmly believing that a serving officer shouldn't profit from war work. And even when he received a £100,000 inventor's award after the war, he gifted most of this money. Whittle was knighted in 1948, and his work was a key com-ponent in producing the de Havilland Comet, the world's first jet airliner, which flew in 1949.

Address Millennium Place, Hales Street, CV1 1JD | Getting there Coventry's main bus station, Pool Meadow, is adjacent | Hours Unrestricted | Tip If engines of any sort are your thing, be sure to drop in to the Coventry Transport Museum, also in Millennium Place, home to the largest publicly owned collection of British vehicles in the world. Plus there's the Midland Air Museum (see ch. 62).

# 39 Garden of Friendship
*Where public art meets public park*

A pretty and manicured mini-maze area lined with box hedging, white gravel and a wooden boardwalk meets the end of the Glass Bridge, which spirals from outside the Coventry Transport Museum in Millennium Place, up and over Lady Herbert's Garden, before returning to ground. This sunken garden is a calm little oasis known as the Garden of International Friendship, and is a popular and peaceful place for city workers to stroll and enjoy the sunshine.

The garden is another product of the Coventry Phoenix Initiative, set in motion in the late 1990s. It was a regeneration project that created a route through Coventry's city centre, on a journey from the past through the present to the future. It starts at the bombed cathedral, passes through Millennium Place and ends at the Garden of International Friendship. The garden is an appealing mix of public art and the thoughtful use of urban space to make for a calm and contemplative area.

The garden was a collaboration between Rummey Design, the landscape architecture and urban design specialist, artist Kate Whiteford, and poet David Morley. Whiteford has described the garden as a 'land drawing', a fragment of a larger maze, while words from Morley's poetry, developed and written through discussions with the local community, are inscribed onto the walls of the garden. The garden is adjacent to Volgograd Place, itself a symbol of international friendship that commemorates Coventry's status as the first-ever city to be twinned with another, after both cities were ravaged by war.

Two arches lead to the garden at the end of a wall made from modern sandstone blocks, which is a nod to the sandstone wall that famously encircled the city during medieval times. The ruins of this medieval wall survive between the two remaining city wall gates from the period, bordering Lady Herbert's Garden, as part of the same conservation area.

**Address** Hales Street, CV1 5FY | **Getting there** Coventry's main bus station, Pool Meadow, is just 200 metres along Hales Street | **Hours** Always open | **Tip** Swanswell Park and Pool, less than 100 metres away, has a tree-lined ornamental pool with fountains, and is a great recreation space right next to the city centre, where you can feed ducks and swans.

# 40 __ George Eliot's Home
*Where the famous writer began to learn her trade*

In 1840, 21-year-old Mary Ann Evans moved with her father to Bird Grove in Foleshill, where she began writing for a newspaper. She would later write under the pen name George Eliot, choosing a male name so her writing would be taken more seriously. *Middlemarch* is her best-known novel, and the fictional Midlands town of the title is said to be based on Coventry. More locally, Foleshill was reflected as the weaving village of Tipton.

Mary Ann Evans was born at South Farm, Arbury Hall, near Nuneaton, just north of Coventry. Her latter school years were spent at Misses Franklin's school in the city, and the school's building, Nantglyn, still stands on Warwick Row. Evans' education was cut short when her mother died, and she returned to the family home to act as housekeeper until she was 21. When her brother, Isaac, became estate manager for Arbury Hall, she moved with her father to Bird Grove in Foleshill. Here she became part of the Rosehill Circle, a group of intellectuals, through family friends Charles and Clara Bray. When Charles bought the *Coventry Herald & Observer*, he asked Evans to write articles and book reviews, which she did anonymously.

The house is an important part of the George Eliot story, but one of Evans' homes that's fallen off the tourist trail. There's nothing to indicate a connection with the writer who lived there for eight years. It was once used as a Bangladeshi community centre, but is currently fenced off and empty. The building has been identified by SAVE Britain's Heritage as being at risk. The organisation has suggested a possible use would be to combine a George Eliot centre with a writing and educational facility. The building is Grade II* listed due to its connection with the writer. The Herbert Art Gallery and Museum has George Eliot exhibits, such as a writing cabinet, pair of leather gloves, and one of Evans' paintings.

Address Bird Grove House, 9 George Eliot Road, CV1 4HT | Getting there 10 minutes on the 6 bus from Pool Meadow station | Hours Always viewable from the outside | Tip By the Foleshill roundabout at junction one of the Coventry ring road stands *Lock Gates*, a sculpture by Ondré Nowakowski. The life-size lock gates are a symbolic entrance to the Coventry canal area, fashioned in oak and steel.

# 41 George Shaw's Tile Hill

*Inspired high-art paintings of housing estates*

Coventry-born artist George Shaw grew up in Tile Hill, a post-war housing estate on the edge of Coventry. It's these two square miles – the streets where he lived until the mid-1980s, when he was 18 years old – that have provided the main subject matter for his acclaimed artwork over the decades. Shaw returned in the 1990s with a camera, capturing images, bound up with memories, upon which he's since based many paintings.

On the surface, Shaw's creations are mundane, yet they're also compelling and unsettling, focusing on bricks and mortar, houses and trees, fences and pavements, yet always devoid of people. Shaw paints with Humbrol enamel, as used by Airfix model makers the world over, and describes his almost photo-realistic artworks as 'suspended between autobiography and fiction'.

Shaw was shortlisted for the prestigious Turner Prize in 2011 for his retrospective *The Sly and Unseen Day*. This included several Tile Hill paintings, such as the local junior school gates, the demolished Massey Ferguson tractor factory, boarded-up shops, and a row of lock-up garages. The awards ceremony took place at the Baltic Centre for Contemporary Art in Gateshead, which was itself designed by another child of Tile Hill, architect Jason Geen. Shaw's failure to win the prize was controversial.

Other Tile Hill paintings include the banana flats at Jardine Crescent, a bus stop and high rise, as well as pubs in the area, locations that can still be seen today. Depicted as crumbling, down at heel and unromantic, the paintings feature man-made non-places on the edge of a city where some would claim there's little to see or do. They're not just snapshots of dilapidated streets however, and collectively they represent more than historical or social documentation. As Shaw once said of his Tile Hill work: 'It grows out of my imagination, my own heart and my own anxieties.'

Address Jardine Crescent, Tile Hill, CV4 9PL | Getting there 25-minute ride on the 6 or 6A bus from Pool Meadow station to Jardine Crescent in Tile Hill | Hours Unrestricted | Tip The Newlands Pub on Tile Hill Lane was built in the Arts and Crafts style in the early 1930s, and includes a pumphouse in the garden.

# 42 GGNP Sikh Temple

*Towering and colourful place of worship*

The Gurdwara Guru Nanak Parkash Sikh Temple is a large, community-funded, multi-faith temple built on Harnall Lane in Coventry in 1996. The towering red-brick building is surrounded by a high wall with blue pillars, and a decorative iron railing on top. Gurdwara means 'door to the guru', and dozens of large Khanda logos – the traditional symbol of the Sikh faith – are fixed to the outer walls, fence and columns. On top of the temple is a huge white dome, featuring a golden ornamental pinnacle.

In 2019, Coventry joined worldwide celebrations of the 550th anniversary of the birth of Sikhism's founder, Guru Nanak Dev Ji. A huge and colourful procession passed through Coventry's streets that November, with trees planted, and a plaque installed in Longford Park. Hundreds of Sikhs also take to the streets every 14 April for Vaisakhi. This is one of the most important dates in the Sikh calendar, commemorating 1699, the year when spiritual leader, warrior and philosopher, Guru Gobind Singh, founded the order of the Khalsa. In a tradition called Nagar Kirtan, men in ceremonial dress lead processions, followed by performers, floats and drummers. Hundreds of Coventrians also attend a flag-changing ceremony at GGNP temple, celebrating Sikh identity and values, during which the Nishan Sahib – a triangular flag on a tall flagpole – is replaced. The steel pole is washed with milk and a new flag in saffron-coloured material is installed. Families come together to celebrate, and sing Sikh hymns.

The temple runs tours in English for schoolchildren and organised groups, and also holds Punjabi classes. Activities available include Sikh martial arts and musical tuition, with Sikh religious education classes in English for children on Saturdays. The langar, or community kitchen of the Gurdwara, serves free vegetarian food to all who enter the temple during the day.

Address 71 Harnall Lane, CV1 4FB | Getting there 7-minute ride on the 20 bus from Pool Meadow station | Hours Daily 4am–8pm, always viewable from the outside | Tip It's just a few minutes' walk along Harnall Lane to the Coventry Canal. A few hundred metres north on the opposite bank is the former Daimler Powerhouse, currently being converted into an artistic hub.

# 43_ Gordon Cullen Tile Mural

*Artistic treat for busy shoppers*

As you pass through the Lidice Entrance into the Lower Precinct shopping area, with its pretty glass canopy, away from the hustle and bustle of the Queen Victoria Road and past the imposing Mercia House tower block, be sure to stop and inspect the Gordon Cullen tile mural. There is a small information board that shares information on the images depicted in the wonderful colours and intricate detail of the ceramic tiles that comprise this public artwork.

Designed in 1958 by architect and artist Gordon Cullen, the mural was commissioned by Coventry's City Planning and Redevelopment Committee on the instruction of the then Chief Architect, Arthur Ling. The painting tells the story of the city, from its early industrial days as a watch, cycle and car manufacturing powerhouse, through to its post-war reconstruction, including the new cathedral designed by Sir Basil Spence, the Belgrade Theatre and Broadgate House. It was originally located at the main entrance to the Lower Precinct, and included maps of both medieval and modern Coventry, depicted in the style of maps from those periods. Sadly these maps were destroyed in the 1970s by careless workmanship, but the rest of the mural was successfully removed from the original location, and transferred to its current home when the precinct was overhauled in 2002.

Wearing his architect's hat, Cullen coined the term 'townscape', which was the title of the book he published in celebration of Coventry, and how people use, inhabit and move through the urban spaces in which they live. Coventry was reportedly the location of the first pedestrianised shopping centre in Europe, and Cullen famously stated: 'There is only one way to enjoy what a town has to offer, and that is the pedestrian's way.' It's the only way to view his Tile Mural too, and you'll have to slow down your stride to take it all in.

Address Lower Precinct, CV1 1DX | Getting there 13-minute walk from Coventry railway station | Hours Unrestricted | Tip Among the Lower Precinct's features is Herbal Inn, part of the longest-running chain of Chinese herbal shops in the UK. It sells traditional Chinese herbal remedies and products such as herbal tea, and offers alternative therapies including acupuncture.

# 44 Home of London Taxis
*Coventry's part in the iconic black cab's rise*

Pictured here is a 2014 TX4 Taxi on show at the Coventry Transport Museum. It was made at London Taxi Company's factory in Coventry's Holyhead Road, where taxis were first made in 1946. Today known as London Electric Vehicle Company, it remains in Coventry, where it makes the iconic London black cab. It's one of the few motor manufacturing firms left in what was once known as Britain's 'motor city'.

The first British car was built in Coventry by Daimler in 1897, after which Coventry's motor manufacturing industry grew until its peak in the 1960s, when the UK was the world's second-largest car producer. Major firms in and around Coventry included British Motor Corporation, which made the Mini, Jaguar, and Rootes Group, which went on to become part of Chrysler, and later Peugeot. Coventry was known as Britain's Detroit, and suffered a similar fate, when in the 1970s and 1980s plants closed as manufacturing shifted overseas. When Jaguar closed its Coventry plant in 2005, London Taxis International was the only remaining firm making vehicles.

Taxi manufacturing came to Coventry when retailers Mann and Overton commissioned Austin Motor Company to design and build a new taxi, the FX. Austin partnered with coach-building company Carbodies, formed in Coventry in 1919, and it was the 1948 Austin FX3 that created the template for the familiar London black cab. London Taxis International was formed in 1985, and in 2006 partnered with Chinese car maker Geely. In 2010 it became London Taxi Company, and was acquired by Geely in 2013. In 2017 it became London Electric Vehicle Company and switched to a £500-million state-of-the-art plant on Ansty Business and Technology Park, becoming the UK's only dedicated electric vehicle manufacturer. Today, it's added a commercial vehicle – a medium-sized van – to its manufacturing line, and continues to produce zero emissions-capable taxis.

Address Millennium Place, Hales Street, CV1 1JD, +44 (0)24 7623 4270, www.transport-museum.com | Getting there Coventry's main bus station, Pool Meadow, is adjacent | Hours Daily 10am–5pm | Tip While at the museum, check out the Sky Blues Bus – a 1973 Daimler Fleetline. The museum acquired this vehicle in 1986, and the following year loaned it to Coventry City FC for their open-top tour after winning the 1987 FA Cup.

# 45 Humber Road Tunnel

*Eerie 1830s' pedestrian subway*

The north and south entrances to the Humber Road Tunnel, which cuts beneath the London to Birmingham railway, are today Grade II-listed in their own right, due to their interesting architectural detail that dates back to the golden age of railways. While interesting, these architectural gems are not the easiest to find. At a bend in the Humber Road next to the Ben Day Care Centre, there's a narrow, surfaced footpath heading south-west from the road. It's fenced on either side for much of the way, and is a little overgrown in places, with trailing brambles, but is easy enough to navigate. Following the path, pass first under a heavily graffitied blue-brick subway beneath the former Coventry Loop Line embankment, then within 150 metres from the Humber Road is the Humber Road Tunnel's north portal. The tunnel itself is around two metres high and two metres wide, and is incredibly dark – perhaps not for those who suffer claustrophobia! Walking through its length of approximately 30 metres creates a strange and disorientating sensation. In fact, visitors might want to bring a torch.

The tunnel dates from 1838, when it was first built as part of the first major wave of railway development in Britain during the Industrial Revolution. It was in the 1830s that the London to Birmingham Railway was established under the guidance of the company's chief engineer, Robert Stephenson, the first line in the world linking major cities.

The tunnel portal itself is constructed from stone, and comprises a central rounded arched opening with retaining walls on either side. Most interesting is the detailing: it has an inner band of zigzag decoration, with an outer band of scalloped mouldings, and the outer wall is capped with large stones. The south entrance to the tunnel carries the exact same detailing, in much the same condition, albeit adorned with graffiti.

Address Near Humber Road, CV3 1LL | Getting there 20-minute ride on the 3 bus from Pool Meadow station, followed by a half-mile walk | Hours Always open | Tip Continue along the footpath, which crosses the River Sherbourne, and after about half a mile joins Shortley Road, opposite the London Road Cemetery (see ch. 57).

# 46 Ira Aldridge Blue Plaque

*Britain's first black Shakespearean actor*

Ira Aldridge, who died in 1867, was Britain's first black Shakespearean actor. 2017 saw Aldridge honoured with a blue plaque in Coventry's Upper Precinct. Aldridge also became Britain's first black theatre manager when he took the role at the Coventry Theatre in 1828, after his acting talents proved a hit with Coventry audiences. So impressed and inspired were they by Aldridge's performances, and the plays he presented at the theatre, that the city petitioned Parliament to abolish slavery, which continued at this time. And all this while Aldridge was still only 20 years of age. In an open letter to Coventrians, he expressed his gratitude that 'Being a foreigner and a stranger are universal passports to British sympathy.'

African-American Aldridge was born in New York in 1807, where he began working as an actor in the 1820s. When his theatre group met with repeated racist attacks, he left New York for England, arriving in Liverpool in 1824. He established himself as the first African-American actor to carve out an acting career outside the US, and over the following years rose to prominence playing leading Shakespearean roles such as Hamlet, Othello, Romeo and King Lear.

The blue plaque commemorating Aldridge was unveiled at the site of the long-demolished Coventry theatre, which was until recently a BHS store. The ceremony was attended by veteran Bermudan film actor Earl Cameron, himself widely celebrated as one of the first black actors to break through in the UK. Cameron's connection to the 19th-century actor lies in the fact that he was trained in acting by Aldridge's daughter, Amanda.

Passed by hundreds, even thousands, of shoppers each day, it's hoped this blue plaque will be a reminder of Aldridge's great achievements, of the persecution he overcame as an African-American, and of Coventry's willingness to welcome people from all over the world.

On this site
stood the Theatre Royal
where the Salvation Army
began its mission
in Coventry on the
17th February
1878.

IRA
ALDRIDGE
(1807-1867)
African American actor
was Manager here of
The Coventry Theatre
in 1828 during the struggle
to abolish slavery
Belgrade Theatre • University of Warwick

B
BRITIS

**Address** The Precinct, CV1 1DD | **Getting there** 11-minute walk along Warwick Row and through the Bull Yard | **Hours** Unrestricted | **Tip** There's a second blue plaque, dedicated to Shakespearean actress Dame Ellen Terry (see ch. 32). This is also in the Upper Precinct, close to the now demolished house where she was born.

# 47 IRA Bombing Memorial

*Commemorating the 'forgotten attack' on a UK city*

The Irish Republican Army (IRA) bomb attack carried out in Coventry city centre in 1939 is often referred to as the 'forgotten attack' on a British city. It's not talked about a great deal, and many Coventrians are even unaware of this dark event in the city's past. Although the clouds of conflict loomed heavy over Britain, and World War II would break out just nine days later, Friday 25 August, 1939 was a market day, and Coventry's Broadgate thronged with people. When the hands of an alarm clock in the carrier basket of a bicycle parked outside Astley's shop struck 2.32pm, a 5lb bomb exploded. Seventy people were injured in the attack, but five lost their lives: Elsie Ansell (21), Rex Gentle (30), John Arnott (15), James Clay (82) and Gwilym Rowlands (50).

The bomb had been planted by the IRA as part of a series of attacks carried out in 1939 and 1940 against English cities, including London, Manchester and Birmingham. The campaign was known as the S Plan, the letter S indicating 'Sabotage', and the focus was on commercial premises. Earlier in 1939, the Coventry terrorist cell had destroyed underground telephone inspection chambers. The bomb was built at James McCormack's lodgings at 25 Clara Street in the Stoke area of Coventry. McCormack and fellow IRA member Peter Barnes were eventually convicted of the bombing, and hanged for their crime. In the months that followed, many Coventrians turned on the city's large Irish community. There were calls for 2,000 Irish factory workers to be sacked, and a protest march against the IRA.

With the onset of World War II, and the Blitz of November 1940 razing much of Broadgate to the ground and seizing the headlines, the IRA bombing of Coventry came to be known as the forgotten bombing. Today, a sandstone monument with plaque stands on Unity Lawn in the grounds of the Cathedral as a memorial to those who lost their lives.

**Address** Unity Lawn, Coventry Cathedral, CV1 5RN | **Getting there** 12-minute walk from Coventry railway station | **Hours** Unrestricted | **Tip** There's a plaque on the wall of the County Hall on Cuckoo Lane, overlooking Unity Lawn, to mark the location of the last public hanging in Coventry: that of Mary Ball who killed her husband by poisoning. The hanging attracted around 20,000 people in 1849.

# 48 Italian Job Plaque

*Marking Coventry's role in the famous heist movie*

The 1969 classic British movie *The Italian Job* featured an unforgettable car chase of Austin Mini cars, which was shot in a Coventry sewer. A plaque marks the spot in Stoke Aldermoor where the vehicles were lowered into the pipe by crane.

The movie tells the story of a Cockney criminal gang that steals gold bullion in a major heist in Turin. They hack into the city's traffic control system to cause gridlock, allowing the thieves to escape with their haul in Mini Cooper S cars. During the getaway, they're chased by police onto the roof of the PalaVela, and a Fiat factory's rooftop test track, before finally shaking off their pursuers by driving into the sewer tunnels. It's one of the most famous and best-loved car chases in cinema history, played out to the track 'Getta Bloomin' Move On!' – more commonly known as 'The Self Preservation Society'.

The sewer tunnel into which the cars escape was actually in the Sowe Valley in Stoke Aldermoor. A camera was mounted to the back of a Mini Moke, followed by the cars as they come close to doing barrel roles within the tight confines of the tunnel, which stretches for around 300 metres. A successful campaign by Coventry local Kevin Conway, to install a commemorative plaque marking the spot where the Minis were lowered into the disused pipes during filming in 1968, came to fruition in 2019, the 50th anniversary year since the film's release.

Among the guests at the unveiling of the plaque were French stunt driver Remy Julienne, who did the driving in the tunnels, and actor David Salamone, who played Dominic, one of the Mini drivers in the movie. Also in attendance was crane driver Neville Goode, who lowered the cars into the sewer pipe, and Joe Whitmore, the local mechanic who'd kept the cars tuned up for the shoot. A trio of red, white and blue minis were also on hand for the event.

**CELEBRATING THE 50TH ANNIVERSARY AND THE LOCATION OF ONE OF THE GREATEST BRITISH FILMS**

## THE ITALIAN JOB

COMMISSIONED BY KEVIN CONWAY & CO
COVENTRYMINICLUB@YAHOO.COM

**Address** near the Barley Lea, CV3 1DZ, where the footpath passes under the A4082 | **Getting there** 20-minute ride on the 3 bus from Pool Meadow station | **Hours** Unrestricted | **Tip** The Millpool on the Hipswell Highway is a great place to eat and drink, and located less than a mile away. It serves good pub grub, and traditional ales from hand-pulled pumps.

# 49 James Starley Statue

*Homage to Coventry's cycle-manufacturing heritage*

A statue of James Starley, father of the bicycle industry, stands alongside the manicured gardens and flowerbeds of Greyfriars Green. It was Starley's Coventry Sewing Machine Company that in 1869 turned to making bicycles, changing its name to Coventry Machinists, and later to Swift Cycle Company. In 1898, the company started to make motorcycles, and in 1900 single-cylinder cars.

After seeing a French-made boneshaker, Starley produced the Ariel in 1871. This was a penny-farthing bicycle with lightweight wire spoke wheels, which soon became all the rage. The large front wheel meant the bicycle went faster for each push of the pedal, as chain-driven bicycle gears had yet to be invented. He also built four-wheeled bicycles, and created chain-drive differential gearing for tricycles – technology that was later the foundation for gearing used in motor cars.

It was Starley's nephew, John Kemp Starley, who in 1888 invented the modern bicycle as we know it today: the Rover Safety Cycle. In contrast to the penny-farthing, this bicycle had similarly sized wheels and a chain-driven rear wheel. It was called the 'safety cycle', as penny-farthings seated the rider very high, with the poor brakes meaning riders of these machines risked falling head first over the handlebars. John Starley's own firm went on to manufacture cars in Coventry under the Rover brand throughout the 20th century. Despite campaigners' efforts, there's no statue to the younger Starley as yet, and the house where he lived on Gloucester Street in Coventry has yet to carry a blue plaque. Coventry commemorated James Starley after his death in 1881, with the unveiling in 1884 of this 20-foot monument in front of a crowd of thousands. The granite memorial features his face and carvings of two of his bicycles – the Ariel penny-farthing and a tricycle – and perched atop is a statue of the Greek god Fame.

**Address** Warwick Row, CV1 1EY | **Getting there** 6-minute walk from Coventry railway station | **Hours** Unrestricted | **Tip** A wonderful abstract 1960s' concrete mural, designed by William Mitchell, is just down the road in the Bull Yard.

# 50 Jamia Mosque

*One of Britain's first Islamic places of worship*

The first mosque – or *masjid* – in Coventry, and one of the first in Britain, the Noorul Islam Jamia Mosque was built on the corner of Eagle Street and George Street in the Foleshill area of Coventry in 1960. Coventry's large industrial and motor manufacturing base at the time made the city a popular destination for Asian immigrants, who began to arrive from Commonwealth colonies after 1948.

Today, the Jamia mosque is run by the Islamic Brotherhood of Coventry, for Muslims to gather for prayer, study and celebrate festivals such as Ramadan. Ramadan is practised in the ninth month in the Islamic calendar – when the holy book, the Quran, was first revealed – during which Muslims abstain from food and drink, smoking and sexual activity during daylight for 29 or 30 days. The end of the fast is marked with the festival of Eid ul-Fitr, when Muslims dress up, visit the mosque for prayer, and visit family and friends for celebration meals.

The Jamia mosque is gated, and is a red-brick building, with doors, windows and roof all featuring cusped arches. The roof is also topped with a pair of white minarets with green domes at their pinnacles, and a larger central green dome with a star and crescent at its summit. There are a number of external inscriptions and calligraphic decorations: *Judge yourselves before you are judged, evaluate yourselves before you are evaluated and be ready for the greatest investigation – the day of judgement.* Also, *Allah says take one step toward me, I will take ten steps toward you. Walk toward me, I will run toward you.*

In a city with a population of more than 400,000, Islam is the second most-followed religion in Coventry after Christianity, and a number of further mosques have been constructed since 1960. The Jamia mosque, now into its seventh decade, remains a pioneering base that continues to serve the Islamic faith in this vibrant and multicultural community area of Coventry.

Address Eagle Street, CV1 4GY | Getting there 10 minutes on the 6 bus from Pool Meadow station | Hours Daily 9am–5pm, always viewable from outside | Tip It's a 4-minute walk to see *Reflections*, the title given to the ceramic and concrete artwork panels by Bhajan Junjan and Naida Hussein. It's attached to the parapet of Priestley's Bridge on Stoney Stanton Road.

# 51 John Parkes Monument

*Unsung burial place of the Coventry gladiator*

In the Cathedral's Unity Lawn at the centre of Coventry, overlooked by the old cathedral's tower and spire, lies an unremarkable monument. It's tucked away, close to the railings that surround the lawn, largely concealed by shrubbery, but can be seen from St Michael's Avenue. The engraving it bears is faded, but it's possible to discern the words: *To the memory of Mr John Parkes, a native of this city. He was a man of a mild disposition, a gladiator by profession, who, after having fought 350 battles, in the principal parts of Europe, with honour and applause, at length quitted the stage, sheathed his sword, and with Christian resignation, submitted to the Grand Victor, in the 52nd year of his life.*

John Parkes, who lived from 1681 to 1733, is buried in the former church graveyard, where a few headstones remain, polished smooth by the elements over the centuries. This particular memorial dates from 1978, supplied by Coventry stonemason Woodheads, and is just the latest replica of the original, which deteriorated beyond repair. Parkes was thought to be a professional sword fighter and fencing master, but was also known as a boxer, at a time when prize fighting was coming into prominence. During his 25-year career as a gladiator he reportedly fought an astonishing 350 contests, many with bladed weapons. He competed a number of times at Bear Garden in Hockley in the Hole in London, where bear baiting and other animal sports took place. In 1710, he was reported in the *Daily Courant* as having issued a challenge to Thomas Hesgate to a fight with back sword, sword and dagger, sword and buckler, falchion and quarterstaff. John Parkes was Coventry's very own Maximus Decimus Meridius!

At the time of writing, there are plans to open up the Unity Lawn space, with new benches and lighting, and all graves and memorial plaques will be preserved and protected.

Address Unity Lawn, Coventry Cathedral, CV1 5RN | Getting there 12-minute walk from Coventry railway station | Hours Unrestricted | Tip Alongside the Unity Lawn are three sublime early-Georgian houses on Priory Row. Number 11 has a distinguished frontage, with six fluted columns.

# 52 John Thornton Plaque

*Tribute to Coventry's Michelangelo of glass*

Half-way along the Burges in Coventry's city centre, on the left as you walk downhill, is a blink-and-miss-it plaque to the man who designed the Great East Window at York Minster. The window remains the largest expanse of stained glass in Britain, in one of Europe's most revered Gothic cathedrals, and is widely referred to as England's own Sistine Chapel. The plaque itself is shaped like the stained-glass window, coming to a pointed Gothic arch.

Coventrian and master glass painter John Thornton lived near the Burges in the early 15th century, and is Coventry's most famous medieval craftsman. His workshop, located in the Burges, was responsible for some of the finest English medieval stained glass, with significant pieces surviving today. His house would have stood partly on what is now the pavement of the Burges, as the route was widened in the 1930s. Records from the time are patchy, but it seems he was active between 1405 and 1433, mostly in Coventry but also in York. It is believed he was recommended for the job that brought him fame by Richard Le Scrope, the then Archbishop of York, and a former Bishop of Lichfield and Coventry. The work was funded by another former Bishop of Coventry, Walter Skirlaw, so he may also have played a role in Thornton's appointment. Thornton was paid a total of £56, with a £10 bonus for on-time delivery – using the Bank of England inflation calculator, that's around £75,000 today.

The Great East Window was constructed between 1405 and 1408, and tells the Christian story of the world from Creation to Apocalypse. It's difficult to imagine the impact this incredible work must have had when it was unveiled to the public in the 15th century. Some examples of Thornton's work can still be seen in Coventry – the new cathedral houses complete Thornton panels in its undercroft, and other pieces survive today in Coventry's Guildhall.

**JOHN THORNTON** Master Glasspainter

John Thornton was the most famous of Coventry's medieval craftsmen. He is best known for designing the Great East Window at York Minster which was constructed between 1405 and 1408 and is the largest expanse of medieval glass in the country.

Coventry was the centre of a flourishing glass-painting industry. John Thornton is known to have lived, and probably worked, near this spot. His house

**Address** The Burges, CV1 1HN | *Getting there* 4-minute walk from Pool Meadow bus station | *Hours* Unrestricted | *Tip* At the time of writing, the charity Coventry Histori Trust is undertaking a project to restore the Burges – one of the few remaining 'high st areas in the city centre, and a prominent shopping and transport thoroughfare dating b to medieval times – by repairing the buildings and shopfronts, and most interestingly, opening up the culverted River Sherbourne on Palmer Lane.

# 53 Lady Godiva Clock

*Mechanical memorial to noblewoman's revealing ride*

The legend of Lady Godiva is one of Coventry's most enduring stories. Godiva was an 11th-century noblewoman, married to the Earl of Leofric. In protest against a heavy-handed tax levy imposed by her husband on his tenants, Godiva rode through the town on a white horse completely naked, her modesty concealed only by her long golden hair. The citizens of Coventry were instructed to remain indoors and not look outside as Godiva passed by. One man, however, was unable to resist the temptation: the famed 'Peeping Tom'. Tom's price for catching a glimpse of Godiva on her bareback protest? To be struck blind for lechery.

For over 65 years, the large clock on the south side of the square in Broadgate has commemorated the story of Lady Godiva's revealing escapade. Between the clock face and the Lady Godiva news kiosk is a balcony, with two doors marked by a black eagle on a yellow background: the symbol of the Earl of Leofric. Every hour on the hour these doors open, and a mechanical wooden sculpture of Lady Godiva on her horse emerges, her golden hair fanning out behind her. As she proceeds, a triangular window opens, and the figure of Peeping Tom leans out, leering at Godiva with his saucer-like eyes, before covering them and withdrawing once more.

The Godiva Clock was moved to Broadgate in 1953 from its original location in the Market Hall Clock Tower, which was rendered unsafe by bombing during World War II. Around the turn of the millennium there was some discussion about replacing the Godiva and Peeping Tom figures with more modern designs, but this was opposed by Coventrians, many of whom consider the original Trevor Tennant sculptures to be modern masterpieces. While some might find the Godiva Clock a creepy, cartoonish spectacle, it's undoubtedly a unique tribute to this Coventry legend, and attracts both locals and tourists alike.

Address 26 Broadgate, CV1 1NE | Getting there 15-minute walk from Coventry railway station | Hours Viewable every hour, on the hour | Tip Check out the Ribbon Factory, built in 1849, that stands in New Buildings, just a 3-minute walk away. It was restored at the start of this century.

# 54 Lady Godiva Statue

*Eye-catching tribute to larger-than-life heroine*

Unveiled in Broadgate in 1949, this tribute to the 11th-century noblewoman Lady Godiva takes pride of place in one of Coventry's busiest pedestrian thoroughfares. The statue depicts Godiva's naked protest against tax demands imposed on the city's inhabitants by her husband, the Earl of Leofric. It's a story that has gathered international significance over the centuries, with Godiva rivalling the warrior Queen Boudica as the best-known medieval British woman. Even today, for many people Lady Godiva remains a figurehead for anti-establishment sentiment.

The huge bronze statue stands on top of a Portland stone base, and was unveiled in 1949 by Peggy Zinsser, wife of the then US Ambassador Lewis Douglas. Indeed, one of the most iconic images of the statue shows its stone base draped in a combined British and American flag. While the sculpture faced south when it was first unveiled, it was turned to face westwards in 1989, when a new shopping complex was built in Broadgate.

The statue was a gift to the city from local businessman William Bassett-Green, and sculpted by Scotsman William Reid-Dick. The memorial cost £20,000 in its day, equivalent to more than £1 million in today's money, and is one of the very few statues that prominently features a horse, outside London, to be Grade II listed. Bassett-Green was a wealthy Coventry businessman, whose grandfather was a major silk ribbon manufacturer in the city. It's said that he contacted Reid-Dick as early as 1936 regarding commissioning of the statue, but the war years intervened, and when the two men had a dispute over the sculptor raising the price in the late 1940s, the project was almost cancelled.

Officially entitled *Self Sacrifice*, it's known by locals as the Lady Godiva statue, and is a favourite resting point for shoppers to stop and sip coffee, as well as one of Coventry's most significant artworks.

**Address** Broadgate, CV1 1NE | Getting there 15-minute walk from Coventry railway station | Hours Unrestricted | Tip Check out the standalone Peeping Tom bust on Hertford Street, above the entrance to the covered walkway – he's an integral part of the Lady Godiva legend.

GODIVA

THEN SHE RODE BACK CLOTHED ON WITH
CHASTITY. SHE TOOK THE TAX AWAY AND
BUILT HERSELF AN EVERLASTING NAME

# 55 Lady Herbert's Garden
*Tranquil retreat in the heart of the city*

Lady Herbert's Garden is an oasis of green in Coventry's city centre, designed to span and complement remains of the city's medieval wall and gates. Work on the garden began in 1930, at the behest of the industrialist Sir Alfred Herbert. He was the man behind Alfred Herbert Limited, one of the world's largest makers and distributors of machine tools.

Herbert bought land in order to create a public flower garden to commemorate his second wife, Florence, who died in May 1930. The garden was completed in 1939, and in its early decades featured a rockery, stream and pools. After Herbert's own death in 1957, responsibility for the garden fell to trustees, and it was subsequently gifted to Coventry City council in the 1970s.

A key aspect of the garden's planning was to safeguard a section of the ruined Coventry city wall, between two surviving gatehouses. Construction of the city wall began in the 14th century, and by the mid-16th century it measured nearly 3.5 kilometres. Consisting of walls around 2.5 metres thick and nearly 4 metres high, it made Coventry the best-defended city in England after London. The walls were demolished by order of King Charles II in 1662, as punishment for Coventry's support for the Parliamentarians during the English Civil War. Those sections of wall within Lady Herbert's Garden are the best-preserved in the city.

The garden's boundaries are marked by sandstone walls around 1.5 metres high, with some railings, gateposts and Gothic buttress bearing the initials FH – for Florence Herbert. Part of the garden is given over to the Lady Herbert's Homes. These almshouses are single-storey cottages built in brick with sandstone details, managed by a charitable trust offering accommodation for elderly retired women. The gardens feature herbaceous borders, shrubs and trees, and it's a popular location for a stroll or picnic.

Address Coventry, CV1 1JQ | Getting there Coventry's main bus station, Pool Meadow, is adjacent | Hours Always viewable from the outside | Tip Opposite Lady Herbert's Garden is the Old Fire Station on Hales Street. Built in 1902, it's largely unchanged since its working life ended in 1976.

# 56  Locarno Murals

*Abstract art at former hit music venue*

The Locarno Dancehall was Coventry's top nightspot in the 1960s and 1970s, and it was here that Chuck Berry recorded his number one hit 'My Ding-A-Ling'. Built in 1958, the dancehall was designed by Donald Gibson's Coventry City Architects department. It was approached by means of a glass staircase tower that connected to the ballroom's second floor, with the two-storey ballroom stretching above shops on the ground floor. The red brickwork remains unchanged, and is criss-crossed with a grid of glass mosaic, featuring the abstract mural work of Fred Millett. Bright colours jump out in the sunlight against a dark background, and it's a fitting visual tribute to the dazzling creativity the storied venue once hosted.

The Locarno was run by the Mecca Leisure Group, and in the early years hosted regular Friday and Saturday dances led by big bands. It wasn't long, however, before jazz and pop acts were involved. The list of live acts that appeared at the venue reads like a who's who of music: The Who, The Small Faces, The Yardbirds, Ike and Tina Turner, and in the 1970s, Pink Floyd and Led Zeppelin. It's also where Coventry-born pop impresario Pete Waterman started out as a DJ. The greatest accolade, however, has to be Chuck Berry's visit on his 1972 British tour, during which the song 'My Ding-A-Ling was recorded live at the Locarno, and featured on his album *The London Chuck Berry Sessions*. The song went on to become a number one single in the UK, and Berry's only number one on America's Billboard Hot 100.

The Locarno changed names to Tiffany's in the mid-1970s, but was converted into the city's central library in 1986, which it remains today. The conversion remained faithful to the original ballroom plan, however, and its double-height dance floor space, with the balcony to the four sides, has largely been retained with the original balustrade.

Address Smithford Way, CV1 1FY | Getting there 13-minute walk from Coventry railway station, 7 minutes from Pool Meadow bus station | Hours Unrestricted | Tip Check out the larger-than-life sculptures representing Coventrians by Trevor Tennant, featured on the Broadgate House Bridge and dating back to 1953, just a 4-minute walk from the Locarno murals.

# 57 London Road Cemetery

*Well-preserved Victorian arboretum graveyard*

The London Road Cemetery, located alongside the major road of the same name, is now recognised by Historic England as one of the top five historic cemeteries in Britain. Despite much-needed repair and maintenance work – which it's receiving thanks to a £1.8-million National Lottery Heritage Fund grant – it's still considered one of the UK's best-preserved Victorian cemeteries.

The Grade I-listed cemetery was created by the famous gardener, architect and MP Joseph Paxton in the mid-19th century. Paxton, who is perhaps best-known today for designing London's Crystal Palace for the Great Exhibition of 1851, was invited in 1845 to design in Coventry what would be one of the country's first municipal burial grounds. The cemetery is the resting place for hundreds of victims of the Coventry Blitz, and notable local figures. These include George Singer, who founded the Singer Cycle Company and whose works football team, Singer FV, went on to become today's Coventry City Football Club, James and John Starley, who invented and produced the bicycle as we know it today, and William 'Paddy' Gill, Coventry's greatest prize fighter, who died in 1869.

Part of the site was a former stone quarry, creating an undulating landscape of mounds and hollows which Paxton incorporated into his cemetery design. Key features include an Italianate lodge at the entrance, an octagonal gazebo, Anglican and Non-conformist Chapels and the Promenade – or Terrace Walk – as well as a dedicated Jewish quarter. The cemetery was originally designed as an arboretum, introducing many new species of trees within its 7-hectare footprint. Mature shrubs and coniferous and deciduous trees give the cemetery a somewhat canopied feel today, making it a good example of an early Victorian garden cemetery. One of the cemetery's key features is the Paxton memorial, a monument designed by Joseph Goddard.

Address London Road, CV1 2JT, +44 (0)24 7678 5492 | Getting there 15-minute ride on the 21 bus from Pool Meadow station, then a 5-minute walk | Hours Daily 8.30am–5pm | Tip It's a 10-minute walk back into town to the Wave, a huge, £36m indoor water park with six main slides that opened its doors in late 2019.

# 58 Lunt Roman Fort

*Reconstructed battlements from 2,000 years ago*

Coventry's Lunt Roman Fort is a partially-reconstructed timber fort, on the excavated archaeological site of a former Roman fort in Baginton, on the south-eastern outskirts of Coventry. The original fort is thought to have been built around the time of the rebellion, led by Boudica against the invading Roman forces, around 60AD. Those early Roman forts were built at speed to shore up areas Romans had fought and won battles and occupied terrain. They were usually constructed from turf and timber first, and later built again from stone when they had to be renewed, and more time and resources were available. The Lunt Fort, however, was never recast as a stone fort, and only occupied for a limited time.

Its location is close to the meeting point of two major and famous Roman roads – Fosse Way and Watling Street – and the original fort would have looked out from its plateau over the River Sowe through Coventry. During excavations of the site over the years, discoveries of Roman armour and equipment for horses point to cavalry units once being stationed at the Lunt. In terms of size and scale, it's estimated that as many as 600 soldiers would have been sited here in the six wooden barrack blocks. The fort was abandoned around 80AD as Roman efforts focused further north on conquering the whole of the British Isles.

A ditch surrounds the fort, behind which was a rampart made of two sloping earth walls, topped with a wooden fence, with gaps for Roman soldiers to thrust their swords at attackers. An interesting feature of the fort is a large, 34-metre ring – a gyrus – which may have been used for training horses.

The site was first identified when quantities of Roman pottery were found in the 1930s, and in the 1970s many of the fort's features were rebuilt upon the original foundations. Today, the fort is open to the public, and is a popular school day-trip destination.

Address Coventry Road, Baginton, CV8 3AJ, +44 (0)24 7623 7575, www.luntromanfort.org | Getting there 20-minute ride on the 17 or 539 bus from Pool Meadow station, then a 13-minute walk | Hours Mon–Fri 10am–3pm | Tip Also in Baginton is Bagot's Castle, a 14th-century ruin, but thought to have been built in the 11th century.

# 59 Lychgate Cottages

*Survivor of the Blitz at Coventry's centre*

These charming cottages, numbered 3, 4 and 5 on Priory Row, next to the entrance next to Holy Trinity Church, were nearly torn down during the city's regeneration after World War II. They were originally one building, known as Lychgate House, but have since been partitioned into three separate cottages. They're named Lychgate after the gate through which coffins were carried into the churchyard to be buried – *lych* derives from the Old English *lic*, meaning corpse.

Timbers used in the building have been dated back to 1415, and many people believe the cottages were sited in front of Coventry's first cathedral, St Mary's Benedictine Priory, founded by Lady Godiva in 1043. Others, however, doubt whether the buildings themselves were constructed then, or built more than 200 years later and simply re-used older timber. This is because they stand on brick barrel-vaulted cellars that were common to the 17th century, and the priory footings were built some four metres lower.

Either way, the half-timbered buildings, with diamond paned glass windows and jettied upper floors, are a wonderful glimpse of Coventry's city centre from centuries ago. Previously private houses, by the mid-19th century they were bought by the neighbouring Blue Coat School, and restored and extended in 1855. The tall chimneys date from this time, as do the internal fireplaces and external stairs. The cottages were then acquired by the council in 1937, and remarkably survived destruction in the 1940 Blitz, that devastated so many of the other buildings in the streets nearby. The cottages underwent restoration work in the late 1990s, and in 2017 were passed on to the Historic Coventry Trust.

At the time of writing, they're scheduled to undergo further specialist restoration, in preparation to be converted into visitor accommodation ready for Coventry's year as UK City of Culture, to begin in May 2021.

Address Priory Row, CV1 5EX | Getting there Coventry's Pool Meadow bus station is a
5-minute walk away | Hours Always viewable from outside | Tip See Graham Sutherland's
huge tapestry, and the stained-glass windows by John Piper, at Coventry's new cathedral,
which is less than 200 metres away.

# 60 Martyr's Memorial Cross

*Commemorating the grim fate of 12 city Christians*

The 6-metre high Martyr's Memorial Cross is a granite monument erected in 1910 to commemorate Lollard Christians who were executed for their beliefs in Coventry in the early 16th century. Lollards opposed the practices of the Catholic Church, felt the Pope had no part to play in worldly affairs, and were supporters of the Bible's translation into English – but they were not a cohesive organisation. The group consisted of seven men and two women, who were executed between 1512 and 1522 during the reign of King Henry VIII, and three further men, executed in 1555 during the reign of Queen Mary. They came from varied backgrounds, including ordinary working men such as shoemakers, glovers and hosiers, as well as a prominent London cleric and a fellow of King's College at Cambridge University.

In 1511, many Lollards appeared before Geoffrey Blythe, the bishop of Coventry and Lichfield. Those who confessed had to renounce their beliefs, but some were later found to have returned to them. Those martyred were burned at the stake in Coventry. The three martyrs executed during the reign of Mary Tudor were charged with continuing to hold Protestant views after she had restored the Catholic faith in England, following Henry VIII's break with the religion. As the inscription on the monument says, the Coventry Martyrs suffered one of the most painful deaths imaginable 'for conscience's sake'.

The monument stands in a public park just outside the Coventry ring road, near to where the executions took place, where Mile Lane meets Quinton Road in Cheylesmore, which was just south of the city wall at the time. In recognition of this dark hour in the city's history, several local streets are today named after the Coventry Martyrs – they include Thomas Lansdail Street, Joan Ward Street, Wrigsham Street, and Silksby Street, after Robert Silksby.

**Address** Junction of Mile Lane and Quinton Road, CV1 2LN | **Getting there** 10-minute walk from Coventry railway station | **Hours** Unrestricted | **Tip** It's a 6-minute walk back into town to admire the Coventry Council House, particularly its clock: it's cantilevered, and its design features the swept-back wings of a golden angel.

# 61_Medieval Spon Street
*Curated collection of historic buildings*

Spon Street boasts a number of wonderful, half-timbered Tudor buildings with jetties that overhang the floor below. However, a visit to Spon Street isn't quite taking a stroll down an untouched medieval lane. While a few old buildings are in their original location, such as the 16th-century Windmill pub, many of the structures on the street were saved from demolition elsewhere in the city, and relocated to Spon Street as part of a scheme that began in 1969. For example, some of the buildings were originally constructed around 1500 on Much Park Street in the city's centre. The last relocation of a building to Spon Street was completed in 1989.

The street's industrial heritage dates back to the 12th century, when it was a hub for dyers, and linked up with Spon End, one of Coventry's oldest areas. Deeds and other records from the time reveal that there were also weavers, saddlers, carpenters and carters active in the street.

By the 19th century, the focus for residents was watchmaking. Indeed, it's on Spon Street that the Coventry Watch Museum is based (see ch. 26). A parade of information boards along the street illustrate these industries, and show what Spon Gate, part of the city walls built in the 14th century, would have looked like in its heyday towards the end of the Middle Ages.

Today, the buildings are protected as part of the Spon Street Conservation Area, and many have visible wooden plaques bearing information about their design, interior layout and heritage. The street includes some excellent examples of Wealden houses: timber-framed hall houses that were more traditional to the south-east of England. One of the best things about the Spon Street buildings, however, is that they're not just a living museum, but house a variety of pubs, specialist shops and eateries, which means that visitors to this historic road can go inside and experience them from within.

Address Spon Street, CV1 3BA | Getting there 13-minute walk from Coventry railway station, along Starley Road and Croft Road | Hours Unrestricted | Tip Walk 3 minutes eastward along Corporation Street and take a look at Jim Brown's concrete sculpture mounted to the Belgrade Theatre's less-glitzy frontage, which symbolises the city of Belgrade.

# 62 Midland Air Museum

*Get up close to historic planes and more*

Midland Air Museum is just outside Coventry's south-east border, alongside Coventry Airport. This plane spotter's paradise is a delightful, self-funded independent aviation museum. It's home to the Sir Frank Whittle Jet Heritage Centre, named after the Coventry-born engineer who famously invented the jet engine (see ch. 38). Exhibits include aircraft, engines – including a Rover-built engine based on a Whittle design that first ran in 1942 – and illustrative materials are on display in a huge aircraft hangar. There's also a second hangar, an Armstrong-Siddeley Gallery, plus an outdoor area where civil and military aircraft are exhibited.

Perhaps the star turn among the museum's 30+ historic aircraft is the Avro Vulcan bomber, originally part of the V bomber force that was designed to carry nuclear weapons during the Cold War. Also on show are a British Aerospace Sea Harrier jump jet, a Boulton Paul, an English Electric Lightning, an MiL Mi4 helicopter, a Lockheed T-33A, and even a MiG fighter. The smallest plane on show is the CMC Leopard, while the oldest jet-powered aircraft in the museum's collection is the Meteor F4, first flown in 1946.

Midland Air Museum was started in 1967 by a small group of local enthusiasts who had collected books, photographs and aircraft parts. The group secured a small plot of land near Coventry airport to host a permanent exhibition, and the museum opened in 1978, with five aircraft on display. The Vulcan bomber joined the exhibits in 1983, and the Argosy freighter in 1987. The World War II Robin Hangar, bought in 1995, provides a covered space for restoration projects and more vulnerable exhibits.

The museum's collection policy is centred on the story of aviation in the Midlands, and Coventry in particular. Videos give a virtual tour through aircraft interiors, and there's also an onsite shop and tea room.

Address Rowley Road, CV3 4FR, +44 (0)24 7630 1033, www.midlandairmuseum.co.uk | Getting there 20-minute ride on the 21 bus from Pool Meadow station, then walk just over a mile | Hours Mon–Sat 10am–5pm, Sun 10am–6pm | Tip A little further along Rowley Road you can try your hand at piloting a Boeing 747 with Flight Simulator Midlands, hosted at Coventry Aeroplane Club.

# 63 Moat House

*Birthplace to Australia's Father of Federation*

The Moat House on Moat House Lane in the Canley area is a Grade II-listed, 16th-century timber-framed and red-brick house that's divided into two cottages. It's significant as the birthplace of Sir Henry Parkes, former Prime Minister of New South Wales in Australia, and the man who many consider to be the Father of Federation there.

In 1815, Henry Parkes was born in this house, which is tucked away in a quiet cul-de-sac off Charter Avenue in Canley. Today it's a private residence, so not open to the public for viewings. He was the youngest child of a tenant farmer on the Stoneleigh Estate, Thomas Parkes, and his wife Martha. When the farm ran into trouble, Parkes began working in a rope factory at the age of 11. At 12, he became an apprentice to a bone and ivory turner. He was a self-educated man who read widely. He joined the Birmingham Mechanics Institute, and also developed an interest in politics, focused on improving conditions for the working classes. He emigrated with his wife to New South Wales in 1839, and after several years in low-paying roles founded the *Empire* newspaper in 1850. In 1854 he was elected to the New South Wales Legislative Council, and led Parliament in 1872. He went on to be a five-time premier of New South Wales, and in later life focused much of his energies into the creation of the Australian Federation. He remains highly revered there, as a politician who helped steer a divided country to nationhood, and also as a champion of women's rights and honest governance.

Parkes was knighted in 1877, and died in 1896, five years before Federation in Australia was finally achieved in 1901. Sir Henry Parkes Road in Canley is named after him in tribute, while in Australia his face was featured on the Australian five dollar note in 2001, in recognition of his pro-Commonwealth activism in the year the country celebrated the Centenary of Federation.

Address Moat House Lane, CV4 8EF | Getting there 15-minute walk from Canley train station, or a 25-minute ride on the 11 or 18 bus from Pool Meadow station, followed by a 5-minute walk | Hours Unrestricted | Tip Much of the housing in Canley is steel-framed, designed and produced by the British Iron and Steel Federation after World War II, with outer walls often clad in steel-trussed sheeting.

# 64   NatWest Bank Doors

*Steel celebration of ancient currency*

The NatWest bank on Coventry's High Street, opened in 1930 as the National Provincial Bank, has a grand fascia with columns that resemble those of a Greek temple. Impressive as these are, the most interesting aspect of the building is its splendid doors, whose detailing is repeated throughout the building.

There is one set of these doors to the main entrance, and another to the side entrance. The main entrance doors fold into a recess during the bank's opening hours, but the side entrance doors are usually closed, and thus on full display. These elaborate doors were designed by the architect W. F. C. Holden, and made by the Birmingham Guild.

Each stainless steel door contains 20 different studded panels, decorated with motifs from coins from around the world through the millennia, including British, Irish, ancient Greek, Egyptian and even Assyrian and Byzantine coins. There's an ear of barley, and panels showing a griffin, a bull and a crab. There are mythical creatures and gods, such as Hercules slaying a lion, Poseidon riding a sea creature, and Apollo fighting a snake. There's a king in a chariot, a lion perched atop a crown, a lyre, and even St. George on horseback slaying a dragon. The detailing of each panel is fabulously intricate, and they're repeated on the plasterwork inside the bank.

Above the main entrance, a line of circular stone carvings also feature coin-inspired symbols, while above the windows of the building are sculptures of different mechanical objects. These are designed to reflect Coventry's most important industries through the centuries, including the inner workings of a watch, a spark plug to represent motor manufacturing, and a differential gear to represent cycling, among many others. The NatWest bank is a fascinating building that rewards the careful and interested observer with many wonderful discoveries.

Address 24 Broadgate, CV1 1NE | Getting there 11-minute walk from Coventry railway station, passing Greyfriars Green and up Hertford Street | Hours Unrestricted | Tip In the foyer of Broadgate House, less than 50 metres away, is the Martyr's Mosaic. This amazing piece of artwork by Dick Hosking depicts 11 Coventry martyrs, burned at the stake in the 16th century.

# 65_Old Bablake School

*Stunning Grade I-listed building*

Bablake School dates back to 1344, when Queen Isabella – widow of King Edward II – gave the Guild of St John the land for a chapel and a college linked to it. Bablake church, now known as St John's (see ch. 78) stands next to the school buildings. In 1560, Bablake School, the building that stands today, was established as a blue-coat school. This was a type of charity school founded in the 16th century for the care and education of poor and abandoned children. They wore blue coats, because blue was the colour associated with charity at the time.

In 1563, former Coventry Mayor Thomas Wheatley made a significant financial contribution to the school by gifting much of his estate. Where his money came from is an interesting story in itself: he ordered some steel from Spain, but as part of the shipment he also received a barrel of silver ingots by mistake. When he was unable to determine the ingots' rightful owner, he gave the money to charity.

Bablake School shared a courtyard with the old Bond's Hospital, itself founded in the early 16th century by another former Coventry Mayor, Thomas Bond. It still operates today as an almshouse, offering charitable housing and sheltered accommodation to the elderly. Together, the two make up a fascinating and historic complex of buildings, which is visible through the arched entrance from Hill Street.

Bablake School continued to occupy the buildings until 1890, at which time it moved to its current location at Coundon Road, leaving the Old Bablake School to function as offices for charities, governors of Bablake School, and the Coventry Schools Former Pupils Association, also known as Bablake Old Boys. The half sandstone, half timber-framed buildings that jetty out onto Hill Street remain beautifully preserved, and a beautiful and much-loved Grade I-listed piece of Coventry architecture.

Address Hill Street, CV1 4AN | Getting there 12-minute walk from Coventry railway station, or 8 minutes from Pool Meadow bus station | Hours Unrestricted | Tip A few minutes' walk away in Lamb Street is a fascinating untitled sculpture by artist John Bridgeman, that stands over 2 metres tall. His best-known piece, the *Mater Dolorosa*, is located in the Lady Chapel in Coventry Cathedral.

# 66 __ Old Cathedral

*Grade I-listed ruin at the city's historic heart*

Coventry's Old Cathedral is a roofless shell, devastated during the Coventry Blitz. As a result, it's known by some locals as the 'cabrio' cathedral. Its real name is St Michael's Cathedral, a Gothic church built in the 14th century but only the outer wall, tower, the 90-metre spire, and the bronze effigy and the tomb of its first bishop survived the bombing. The day after the Blitz, demolition crews were reportedly halted from pulling down the leaning Cathedral tower, which survived the bombs but was leaning precariously: they didn't realise it had been leaning for a least 100 years!

A notable feature of the cathedral is the Charred Cross, which was created when cathedral stonemason Jock Forbes found wooden beams lying in the shape of a cross after the bombing. It also contains a bronze cast of the statue *Reconciliation* by Josefina de Vasconcellos, which was presented to the cathedral in 1995 to mark the 50th anniversary of the end of World War II. The words *Father Forgive* were inscribed on the wall behind the altar after the war. The cathedral has not been restored, in commemoration of the events of 1940. However, a new, modernist Cathedral, the Cathedral Church of St Michael, was built alongside the original structure, using the same sandstone. It's a spot that's popular with office workers at lunchtime, and plays host to live music and theatre events, food and drink festivals, and recently an ice-skating rink for the first time.

After the Blitz bombing raids, Germany's Minister of Propaganda, Joseph Goebbels, used the term *coventriert* – or 'coventried', meaning totally devastated – to describe the impact of similar raids on other towns.

The bombing did not put an end to reports of St Michael's Tower being home to a ghost, while there have been reports that the cellar beneath the Tourist Information Office on the tower's ground floor is haunted.

**Address** Priory Street, CV1 5FB, www.coventrycathedral.org.uk | **Getting there** Coventry's main bus station, Pool Meadow, is less than 200 metres away | **Hours** Always viewable from outside | **Tip** Around 100m from the Old Cathedral, Holy Trinity Church houses a stunning painting of the Last Judgement – it's above the tower arch and is known as the Coventry Doom.

# 67 Old Grammar School
*Splendid historic sandstone building*

Coventry's Old Grammar School is a Grade I-listed building, and in its former incarnation as the chapel of St John's Hospital, the building on this site dates from the 12th century. The building, which sits on the corner of Bishop Street and Hales Street, was surrendered to the crown during the dissolution of the monasteries under King Henry VIII, and sold to John Hales, with the stipulation that he set up a grammar school in the city.

Sure enough, the former hospital chapel became a Free Grammar School for Coventry's children – 15th-century oak choir stalls were brought in and used as desks, and remain in the building today. The building lost its half-timbered library when the Burges, Coventry's main transport route, was widened in 1794. Part of the west end of the old church, and its bell tower, were also demolished the same year. It remained a grammar school until its pupils were moved in 1885 to a larger, 13-acre site on Warwick Road, where it still stands today as King Henry VIII Grammar School.

A £1.5-million restoration was completed in 2015, as part of work on the adjacent Coventry Transport Museum, after standing empty for some 20 years. A lot of stonework was replaced, a new floor installed, and heating introduced for the first time. The fine Gothic east window was replaced with diamond pane glass, although it would once have been a stained-glass window. The work breathed new life into this ancient sandstone building, and was highly commended in the 2016 Civic Voice Design Awards. Since then it has been used as a venue for events such as conferences and weddings, and has played host to the Coventry Business Improvement District team – a partnership between the businesses located within the ring road of Coventry city centre. Otherwise public access has been mainly limited to Coventry's annual heritage weekends, which usually fall in September.

Address Hales Street, CV1 5EX | Getting there 3-minute walk from Pool Meadow bus station | Hours Always viewable from outside | Tip Just a few minutes' walk up the Burges brings you to Broadgate and the splendid Cosy Club. With a baroque bar and nostalgic gentlemen's club feel, be sure to check out the extensive cocktail menu.

# 68 PC Gavin Carlton Memorial

*Tribute to officer whose murder shocked the nation*

On 19 December, 1988, two armed men held up Coventry's Tile Hill branch of the Midland Bank, demanding cash. This set in motion a chain of events that saw a police officer killed in the line of duty.

When the raid began, a bank clerk pressed a panic button, and PC Gavin Carlton was first on the scene. As the criminals made their escape he gave chase in his police car, and followed their vehicle into nearby Torrington Avenue. They fired a sawn-off shotgun, which caused him to crash into a bollard on the pavement. As PC Carlton tried to reverse, the gunman killed him with a single shot at point-blank range. PC Carlton was just 29 years old.

Resuming their getaway, the robbers' vehicle was rammed by another police car on Coventry's A45, and following a struggle a second officer, DC Len Jakeman, was also shot and injured. The gunmen fled on foot and took refuge in a house in Earlsdon. A siege ensued, with 20 police marksmen surrounding the residence. One of the criminals, Nicholas Hill, surrendered, and was later sentenced to 14 years in prison; his accomplice, David Fisher, took his own life during the siege.

In 1990, PC Carlton was posthumously awarded the Queen's Commendation for Brave Conduct. A memorial was unveiled at the spot in Torrington Avenue where he fell, attended by the then Home Secretary David Waddington, the Chief Constable of West Midlands Police, and the movie director Michael Winner, who was at that time Chairman of the Police Memorial Trust. A short commemorative service takes place each year. A plaque at Coventry Central Police Station describes the officer as: *A modest, decent, honourable man who will forever live in our hearts because of the gallantry shown at the time of his death. By that he became wholly outstanding. He was an exemplary example, a shining inspiration to us all.*

Address Torrington Avenue, CV4 9HN | Getting there 15-minute walk from Tile Hill railway station | Hours Unrestricted | Tip The distinctive St Oswald's Church in nearby Jardine Crescent features an eye-catching modernist concrete bell tower, designed by Sir Basil Spence. Locals either love or hate this construction, which visitors often mistake for a fire station drill tower.

# 69 Philip Larkin Plaque

*Poem for Coventry by famous British writer*

There's a Coventry Heritage Plaque at Coventry railway station, mounted on a wood-panelled wall above a number of other signs, visible on platform one. It quotes the opening lines of the poem *I Remember, I Remember* by Philip Larkin, who was born in Coventry in 1922, and is widely considered to be one of Britain's most talented 20th-century poets.

The poem's narrator is on a train that stops unexpectedly at Coventry station, and is reportedly based on a trip Larkin himself took in 1954. The narrator comments to his companion that he was born in Coventry, and puts his head out of the window, seeking a nostalgic view of the station from which he'd set off on many family holidays. Reading the plaque, the poem would seem to represent a celebration of a man returning to his roots, but the poem takes a very different turn.

Larkin was born in the Radford area of the city before moving to Cheylesmore, location of the family home for 14 years, before it was demolished in the 1960s to make way for the city's ring road. He was educated at King Henry VIII School on Warwick Road, where he contributed to the school magazine *The Coventrian*. After he left for St John's College at Oxford, Larkin rarely returned. Larkin's father Sydney was reportedly a tyrant and a Nazi sympathiser, so Larkin's childhood in the city wasn't the happiest. In the poem, he describes this time as 'unspent', in a place where nothing happened – Coventry was just where he started out. The poem's narrator imagines an idealised childhood instead, and realises he would likely have been an unhappy child wherever he was. The sentiment feels true to Larkin's image as a famously melancholic writer.

Coventry railway station is today a listed building, and while *I Remember, I Remember* isn't kind to the city, as the plaque states, its author remains nonetheless, *Philip Larkin, Poet and Coventrian.*

Address Station Square, CV1 2GT | Getting there 9-minute ride on the 12X or X17 bus from Pool Meadow station | Hours Always viewable from Platform One | Tip Check out the red-brick King Henry VIII school where Larkin was educated. It's just a 5-minute walk south from Coventry railway station.

# 70_Playwrights
*Stylish independent bar and bistro*

Playwrights is an independently-owned bar and bistro within a listed building on Hay Lane, one of the medieval cobbled streets at the heart of Coventry's historic Cathedral Quarter. Opened in 2001, Playwrights produces its meals fresh on the premises, using ingredients sourced from a variety of local suppliers.

Playwrights occupies the ground floor of a late 18th- or early 19th-century red-brick, three-storey building with sash windows. The ground floor has a double shop front, with wood paned window frames, so interior diners get an uninterrupted floor-to-ceiling view onto the cobbled streets and its al fresco diners. The venue's glass frontage gives the entire establishment a very light, open and airy feel.

There's a full *à la carte* menu on offer, with main courses including lamb shank, steak, salmon fillet and burgers. There's also a cooked breakfast menu, full hot or cold lunches, and a dedicated Sunday lunch menu. There's also a variety of mains for vegetarians or vegans, and clear guidance for those on gluten-free diets. Playwrights' small bar serves a range of beers, wines, spirits and soft drinks. It all adds up to a very inclusive experience for customers regardless of their dietary requirements.

There's plenty of seating out on the cobbled streets when the weather is fair, in sight of the lovely Golden Cross pub (see ch. 92), all just around the corner from the New and Old Cathedrals. Inside Playwrights there are sofas near the bar area, wooden chairs and tables in the dining area, with separate nooks for those seeking a little privacy. The interior décor is a celebration of the city's Cathedral Quarter, with plenty of artful images of historic Coventry, including a large black and white panoramic image of the Old Cathedral along the back wall. A second Playwrights café opened in August 2020 at Coventry's Canal Basin.

**Address** 4–6 Hay Lane, Cathedral Quarter, CV1 5RF, +44 (0)24 7623 1441, www.playwrightsrestaurant.co.uk | **Getting there** 13-minute walk from Coventry railway station via Hertford Street, or 5-minute walk from Pool Meadow bus station | **Hours** Tue–Thu 10am–9pm, Fri & Sat 10am–10pm, Sun 10am–6pm | **Tip** Less than 5-minutes' walk away along Hertford Street is the Yard, an award-winning LGBT+ bar and late-night venue.

# 71 Renold Chains Memorial

*Coventry firm's tribute to fallen employees*

As you enter the Spon End area from the west, turn left just before the dramatic arches of the blue-brick viaduct, and within 50 metres you'll encounter a statuesque and storied war memorial, painted black and towering at around 3 metres in height. Built by Coventry Chain Company – which manufactured bicycle chains for this booming industry at the end of the 19th century, and later track chains for use in tanks during World War I – the monument was originally in the form of a drinking fountain and horse trough. It was presented to the city by the managing director of Coventry Chain in 1920, and was sited on the city's Hearsall Common green space as a memorial to the company's 45 employees who were killed in World War I. The names are listed alphabetically on the memorial, from H. Anderton to C. Wilson.

Over the years the horse trough and the wrought iron sides of the fountain were removed, and the monument was finally taken down. However, the column was restored to something like its original glory, and was rededicated in 1999 to this new location, in front of the Koco building, which is today a community resource centre.

In 1930, the Coventry Chain company merged with another chain-maker, Hans Renold, to become the Renold and Coventry Chain Co, which later became Renold Chains. Where the memorial stands today is outside the former Renold Chains factory office building in Spon End. Intriguingly, the shield-shaped dedication plaque – which reads *Erected by the employees of the Coventry Chain Co in memory of their 45 comrades who fell in the Great War 1914-1918* – was separated from the column, but found in a market in Lancashire, and re-fixed to the monument. Renold Chains also has a separate memorial plaque inside the Cenotaph in Coventry's War Memorial Park (see ch. 108), erected to those company employees who served their country in both World Wars.

Address Arches Industrial Estate, CV1 3JQ | Getting there 7-minute ride on 6A, 14 or 18 bus from Pool Meadow station | Hours Unrestricted | Tip A half-mile walk east brings you to Artspace, at 16 Lower Holyhead Road, formerly the Holyhead Youth Club. Here, a plaque reveals that this is where many members of Coventry 2-Tone bands The Specials and The Selecter first met.

# 72 Replica Civil War Cannon

*Check out the big gun when shopping*

There's a replica Civil War cannon – a saker field gun from 1645 – at the road entrance to Cannon Park shopping centre. It's dedicated to GNR Harry Norman Fletcher of the Second Searchlight Regiment Royal Artillery for duties during World War II. It's also a reminder of Coventry's role in the English Civil War, from 1642 to 1651.

Cannons were a key part of Coventry's defence, firing iron balls and stones. The financial and religious policies of King Charles didn't sit well with Coventrians. Society divided into those who would support the king, known as Royalists or Cavaliers, and those who would not, known as Parliamentarians or Roundheads, with Coventry very much in the latter camp. In 1642, William Jesson – a dyer, former Mayor of Coventry and then Member of Parliament – went to London to purchase cannons to defend the city in the looming Civil War. At the war's outset, the Earl of Northampton reportedly bombarded the city wall for days, with little success. Where the wall was breached, Coventrians stopped up the gaps, and while many dozens of Royalists were killed, only one inhabitant of the city is said to have died. The King's Nephew, Rupert Rhine, was repelled by 26 cannons when he tried to attack Coventry, and the city became a Parliamentarian stronghold.

Lord Brooke and Robert Devereux, Earl of Essex, managed the defence of the city against attack in the Civil War's early years. At times the city reportedly held 4,000 troops and had its own militia. Oliver Cromwell visited Coventry on a number of occasions, and wrote letters to conduct his campaigns from the city. After his father's execution in 1649, King Charles II restored order with the Restoration of the monarchy in 1660. He ordered Coventry's medieval walls to be pulled down, as they were a symbol of resistance. Only small sections remain, along with reminders such as this replica cannon.

**Address** Cannon Park Centre, Lynchgate Road, CV4 7EH | **Getting there** 25-minute ride on the 11 or 12X bus from Pool Meadow station | **Hours** Unrestricted | **Tip** Nearby Gibbet Hill was the site of a scaffold for public hangings, known as a gibbet, used for executions in the city from the mid-16th century.

# 73_Rotunda Café

*Mushroom-shaped coffee shop is an iconic landmark*

Plans for the overhaul of Coventry's outdated medieval city centre were underway even before the bombings of World War II. Donald Gibson, who headed up Coventry Council's City Architects Department, was already drafting revolutionary architectural designs to modernise the town centre, and the events of the Coventry Blitz only accelerated his efforts. One of the signature pieces of this vision was Coventry's new, fully pedestrianised shopping precinct, the architectural star of which remains largely unchanged to this date: the Rotunda Café.

The glass-sided café opened in the 1950s, since when it has been one of Coventry's most recognisable landmarks. As a Wimpy Bar restaurant for many of those years, in the 1990s the café came under threat when councillors wanted to demolish it as part of wider plans to revamp the Lower Precinct shopping area. The café was saved following the intervention of English Heritage, which endorsed it as a prime example of post-war development, and said it must be kept intact. Today, any planned changes to the Rotunda Café must include consultation with Coventry Council and English Heritage. The architects of the latest iteration of the Lower Precinct have described the Rotunda as a 'Fabergé Egg' that has great prominence within the current atrium space. It is referred to perhaps a little less fancifully, but with plenty of affection, by many of Coventry's citizens as the 'mushroom café' and the 'flying saucer' due to its shape.

The café has been home to a Caffè Nero for several years, but remains a unique venue offering an unparalleled view of the Lower Precinct. This makes it perfect for shoppers and those on a lunch break who like to sit and watch Coventrians going about their business. However, visitors who enjoy a long, leisurely coffee break should note that despite its offer of beverages, the café has no toilets!

Address Lower Precinct, CV1 1DX, +44 (0)24 7623 1050 | Getting there 13-minute walk from Coventry railway station; Lower Precinct parking | Hours Mon–Sat 6.30am–7.30pm, Sun 8am–6.30pm | Tip Fans of independent coffee shops should pay a visit to Myrtle's on Albany Road in Earlsdon, less than a mile away – a lovely little café with friendly staff.

# 74 Sgt Bilko's Emporium

*Museum that keeps the spirit of Phil Silvers alive*

This store in the heart of FarGo Village specialises in cult film and TV memorabilia, taking its name from the Emmy Award-winning 1950s' TV show *Sgt Bilko*. At the back of the store is the Phil Silvers Museum, dedicated to the actor made famous in the title role, featuring a carefully curated display of personal items.

Set in Fort Baxter, a US Army post in the fictional town of Roseville, Sergeant Bilko runs the motor pool – the army fleet of vehicles – and over more than 140 episodes spent his time devising get-rich-quick schemes. *Sgt Bilko* spawned the TV cartoon *Top Cat* in homage to the show, which was broadcast in the UK until 2004, and the Emporium is a labour of love for owner and *Bilko* fan Steve Everitt.

Everitt has collected Phil Silvers memorabilia for over 35 years, since discovering the show in the 1980s. Silvers himself gave his blessing to Everitt's Coventry-based Phil Silvers Appreciation Society – launched in 1984 with friend Mick Clews. Everitt was even invited onto the BBC's *Pebble Mill at One* TV programme to talk about the society, which included a personal recorded message from Silvers. Everitt opened the store and museum on 1 November, 2015, on the 30th anniversary of Silvers' death. Visitors have since included celebrity Silvers enthusiasts such as Danny Baker, Tim Vine and Paul Merton. Mark Hamill – aka *Star Wars*' Luke Skywalker – has tweeted thanks to Everitt for his efforts to keep the Silvers name alive.

Many of the museum's exhibits have been donated by Phil's daughter Tracey Silvers, and other family members. On show is Silvers' driving licence from the early 80s, a pair of glasses he wore during the show, a velvet smoking jacket, and original artwork from the show's title sequence, as well as countless letters, books and photographs. In time, Everitt would like to turn the store into the Phil Silvers Comedy Museum.

Address Fargo Village, Far Gosford Street, CV1 5ED, www.sgtbilkosvintageemporium.com |
Getting there 25-minute walk from Coventry railway station, 8 or 13 bus to Far Gosford
Street | Hours Daily 10am–6pm, Fri 10am–7pm, Sun 11am–4pm | Tip Far Gosford Street
is lined with fast food eateries selling cuisine from all over the world. The Pasha Turkish Grill
does a great job of Mediterranean, Turkish and Middle Eastern meals to eat in or take away.

# 75 Shree Krishna Temple

*White-domed feature of Coventry's skyline*

The Shree Krishna Temple – or to give it its full name, Shree Gujarati Hindu Satsang Mandal – is a fascinating, elaborate place of Hindu worship that opened in Coventry in 1992. After recent development work, it now features a number of domes, and detailed sculptures from India.

The Shree Krishna Temple runs regular tours of its interior wonders, encouraging schools and scout groups to visit and gain a fuller understanding of the Hindu faith and culture, and Hinduism's belief in Brahman as a supreme God. Hindus worship in a temple called a *mandir*, which can vary from small village shrines to large buildings such as the Shree Krishna Temple, which contains beautifully decorated shrines to the Hindu gods. The temple holds weekly *bhajans* – the singing of spiritual songs to help quiet the mind and open the heart to the divine.

The temple runs a school teaching Gujarati, the language widely spoken in Western India, to all age groups. It also teaches the Vedic culture, the religion of the ancient Indo-European-speaking peoples who entered India about 1,500 years before the common era, which takes its name from the collections of sacred texts known as the Vedas. Vedism was one of the major traditions that shapes Hinduism today.

The Shree Krishna Temple prides itself on being a thriving community hub. As well as religious activities and cultural classes, there are music classes and activities to maintain physical health, including dancing. Hindus believe life is a cycle of birth, death and rebirth, and in karma – that is, what happens in the next life depends on how the previous life was lived. There is morning and evening worship, and *arti*, in which lights are waved as a sign of humility and gratitude, and large annual events such as Diwali, the Indian festival of lights, which is celebrated with carnival stilt-walkers, drummers and illuminated floats.

Address Hamall Lane, CV1 4EZ, www.sktcoventry.org.uk | Getting there 7-minute ride on the 20 bus from Pool Meadow station | Hours Daily 9am–noon, always viewable from outside | Tip A 5-minute walk along Foleshill Road and on to Leicester Row will bring you to an interesting work of art called the Wavy Seat, situated alongside the canal, about 50 metres north of bridge number one.

# 76 Spon End Arches
*Vaulted blue-brick viaduct with a history*

Visitors approaching Coventry city centre from the west on the Allesley Old Road will pass through the atmospheric blue-brick Spon End arches. This railway viaduct has stood since 1859 at the mouth of Spon End, which is one of Coventry's oldest areas.

Spon End dates back to the 12th century, and was the main approach to the city from England's northern towns. It was settled by weavers and dyers, who relied on the River Sherbourne, now culverted beneath the city, to carry out their trade. The area was connected to the city centre by Spon Street, and when the city wall was built in the 14th century, Spon Street was the location of one of the gates. The Coventry to Nuneaton railway runs through Spon End over an arched viaduct that's a quarter of a mile long. This was built by the London and North Western Railway, and opened in September 1850. Just a handful of years later, however, on 26 January, 1857, 23 of the 28 sandstone arches of the Spon End viaduct collapsed. The *Coventry Herald* said in 1857: '...the accident was caused in consequence of the foundations of the arches having given way.' Fortunately this happened in the early hours of the morning when the line was not in use and the streets below were unoccupied. Replacement arches were built from strong and damp-proof blue engineering bricks, and the line was reopened in October 1860. Today the Coventry to Nuneaton line has a passenger service that has been much improved in recent years, and is also used by freight trains to avoid passing through Coventry station.

Spon End's blocks of flats, high rises and other post-war social housing are mixed with much older buildings, with the view through the arches revealing this interesting mix. The space beneath the viaduct is now occupied by The Arches Industrial Estate, home to a variety of firms related to motoring and fitness, plus a snooker hall and bar.

Address Spon End, CV1 3HF | Getting there 7-minute ride on the 6A, 14 or 18 bus from Pool Meadow station | Hours Unrestricted | Tip Pass through the arches towards the city centre, and you'll encounter the Butts Park Arena on Butts Road, home to Coventry Rugby Club. Their names are reputedly derived from the sport of archery, which King Edward IV made compulsory on Sunday and holidays in the 15th century, the word 'butt' referring to a target.

# 77 — St Chad Bell Tower

*Skeletal but statuesque concrete construction*

This Grade II-listed concrete church and eye-catching modernist tower in Wood End are arguably in the best condition of three around the city that were designed by Basil Spence, and built by Wimpey in the mid-1950s.

The three church designs were commissioned by Bishop Gorton of Coventry, and many of the experimental ideas would be used by Spence in the construction of Coventry's new cathedral. It was a technical innovation for the time, featuring no-fines concrete, which eliminated sand from the regular concrete mix. Instead, the coarse aggregates in the mix are held together by cement paste to give the strength of concrete, but with a lower density and lighter weight. Demand for post-war housing was very high, and Wimpey was known for producing houses quickly and cheaply, reducing the need for in-demand skills such as bricklaying. The technique hadn't been used on such large-scale buildings before, however.

Bishop Gorton used the money that the diocese had received from the War Damages Commission as compensation for the Blitz to commission Spence's design for three churches, each of which would have a community hall and a bell tower. As well as St Chad's in Wood End, there was also St Oswald's in Tile Hill, and St John the Divine in Willenhall. The cost for the three churches was £50,000, and the funds would only have paid for one similar-sized church built with more traditional brickwork.

The most interesting feature, however, is the bell tower. It's made from reinforced concrete and cedar-wood, and links to the church at its base via a covered walkway. The tower is really a skeleton, with reinforced concrete corner posts and lintels, while its ceiling has a cross of concrete beams, to anchor a central bell, although there is no bell in place. Atop the platform is a steel cross. It really is a striking interpretation of a church tower.

Address Hillmorton Road, Wood End, CV2 1FY | Getting there 20-minute ride on the 21 bus from Pool Meadow station | Hours Unrestricted | Tip Just a few minutes away is a stretch of the Potters Green Corridor, a section of which is the green space of Moat House Park.

# 78 St. John the Baptist

*Stunning church that spawned a famous saying*

Located in medieval Spon Street, St. John the Baptist Church is a Grade I-listed medieval place of worship dating from the 14th century, and which is today in the Church of England Diocese of Coventry. Following the death of King Edward II, his widow, Queen Isabella, gave the parcel of land to the Guild of St. John the Baptist to build a chapel for prayer.

The church closed with the Dissolution of the Monasteries, after King Henry VIII became head of the Church in England and split from the Pope in the 1540s. Then, during the English Civil War of 1642–1651, the church was used to house Scottish Royalist prisoners after the Battle of Preston. Coventrians supported the Parliamentarians, so gave the prisoners the cold shoulder. This is where the well-known saying 'sent to Coventry' originated, meaning to ignore or shun someone.

St. John the Baptist was finally restored as a parish church in 1734. Its nave, aisles, central tower and chapels remain, as do flying buttresses and parapets added in the late 19th century. Today, visitors travel long distances to admire the stained-glass windows, altarpieces, ornate medieval carvings, reredos and green men. Intriguingly, however, most visitors spend more time photographing the brass plate that sits beneath the west window, commemorating the terrible conditions of the winter of 1900, which reads: *This plate marks the height of the water which flooded this church on Dec 31st, 1900.*

The church is also home to a famous relic of St. Valentine of Rome, a reliquary containing a fragment of bone reportedly from St. Valentine himself, with a wax seal as a stamp of authenticity. This is normally kept locked away from public view, however, and is rarely displayed. Behind the church is a small burial ground, which offers very good views of the timber-framed Old Bablake School and Bond's Hospital from the 14th century.

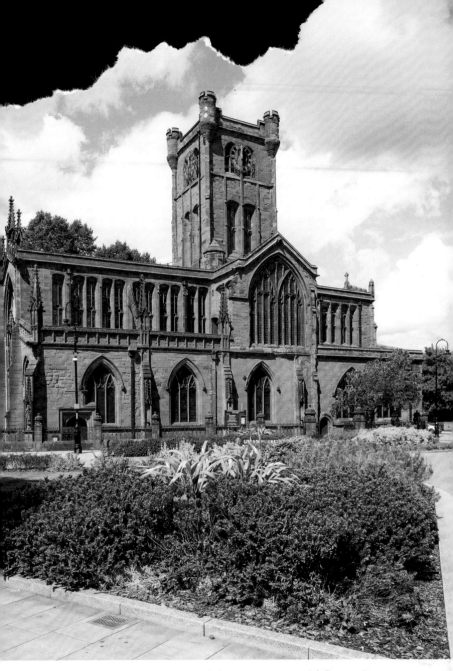

Address Fleet Street, CV1 3AY, www.stjohnthebaptistcoventry.org.uk | Getting there
12-minute walk from Coventry railway station, 8 minutes from Pool Meadow bus station |
Hours Unrestricted | Tip A short walk up Hill Street then Bond Street will bring you to
the Town Wall Tavern. The pub sign depicts the medieval city wall, and inside is one of the
country's smallest snugs, measuring just six feet square.

# 79 St Mary's Priory Ru

*The first of Coventry's three cathedrals*

The remains of the only English cathedral destroyed in the Protestant Reformation are now part of an urban garden at the heart of Coventry. Today, a heritage centre has been built on the ruins of Coventry's first cathedral, St Mary's Priory and Cathedral. This was destroyed during the dissolution of the monasteries, and lay hidden until its ruins were uncovered in 1999 following a dig by Channel 4's *Time Team* archaeologists, supported by the city council. The team also found a 14th-century wall painting and relics from nearly 1,000 years of Coventry's history.

St Mary's was built shortly before its sister church in Lichfield, which was also part of the same diocese, and was believed to have been completed by the early 13th century. The ruins of Coventry's first cathedral, originally founded by Earl Leofric and Lady Godiva, were buried beneath the city centre for hundreds of years. This was the case until the removal of a 1950s' church hall built on top of the St Mary's Priory ruins led to the remains of the Priory being revealed in a garden. The Priory Garden is sited in the nave of the original Benedictine Priory, and is a wonderful place to wander and relax. An artwork laid out in the excavated remains of the garden by Christine Browne depicts Cofa's Tree. This refers to a tree planted by or named after Cofa that marked the original settlement in this area. It's thought to be the most likely source of the city's name.

The garden has a gravelled central area with shrubs around the edge and paved paths at the perimeter. The lower courses of the walls of the original cathedral are visible, and there are six glass boxes within the Priory Gardens, displaying fragments of stone found during the excavations. A wooden footbridge affords a good aerial view of the priory's footprint. Next to the gardens is the Priory Cloister and visitor centre.

Address Priory Row, CV1 5EX | Getting there Coventry's Pool Meadow bus station is a 3-minute walk away | Hours Unrestricted | Tip Just 100 metres away, in the Cathedral Lanes shopping complex, is The Botanist – a cocktail bar with impressive botanical displays, bridges over water features, and potted plants. It has a secret garden feel, and a stunning glass ceiling offering views of the church spire.

# 80 St. Michael Sculpture

*New cathedral's Victory over the Devil*

*St. Michael's Victory over the Devil* is a bronze sculpture mounted on the east wall of the new Coventry Cathedral, next to John Piper's stained-glass window. Standing nearly eight metres tall, a winged St. Michael as avenging angel with arms outspread, spear in hand, adopts a victorious stance above the prostrate figure of the horned Devil, arms and feet bound, looking up in submission. From the steps leading up to the cathedral from Priory Street the statue is almost within arm's reach, announcing the entrance to both the old and new cathedrals of St. Michael. Referenced in the Old Testament and in Catholic writings, St. Michael the Archangel is the iconic defender of the Church against the Devil, the imagery symbolic of the victory of good over evil.

This magnificent sculpture was produced by Jacob Epstein in 1958. Epstein was born in New York to Polish-Jewish parents, and had a reputation for controversial work that disrupted conventions. In commissioning the work, the new Cathedral's architect, Sir Basil Spence, and Bishop Neville Gorton, had to overcome objections to Epstein's unorthodox style. Interestingly, the angel could have ended up with the face of the famous British artist Lucian Freud. Epstein used two models, both of whom were husbands to his daughter, Kitty, who was married to Freud for five years before marrying economist Wynne Godley. It's Godley's face that won the beauty pageant to become St. Michael. Many observers believe the devil's face may be based on a grimacing and bulging-eyed version of Epstein's own features.

Sadly, the sculpture was one of the last major works of art Epstein produced. His death in 1959 meant that he missed seeing the statue finally unveiled in 1961, a ceremony performed by his widow, Kathleen. Today it remains one of the most striking and immediately identifiable features of Coventry's new cathedral.

Address Priory Street, CV1 5FB | Getting there Just 200 metres from Pool Meadow bus station | Hours Unrestricted | Tip Also check out *The Coventry Boy* statue, across the road from the cathedral – Philip Bentham created this model of a young man brandishing a roll of paper to celebrate his apprenticeship, as a shrine to social mobility.

# 81 Stanislaus Kostka Church
*Hub for Coventry's Polish population*

St Stanislaus Kostka Church on Springfield Road in Foleshill is a Roman Catholic Church that serves the city's large Polish population. St Stanislaus Kostka was a Polish novice of the Society of Jesus, a religious order of the Catholic Church with its headquarters in Rome. He was born in 1550 and died in 1568, and canonised in 1726.

The Polish Catholic community in Coventry began organised worship in 1948, with services at the church of Christ the King, and later from St Mary's Church in Raglan Street. The Polish community at that time consisted mainly of veterans of the Polish Armed Forces in the West, so services were held in English churches. But as the Polish community in Coventry grew in the post-war years, so did the desire for a dedicated Polish church. After years of community fundraising efforts, St Stanislaus Kostka opened in 1961 at the junction of Harnall Lane and Springfield Road – a very short walk from the Shree Krishna Hindu Temple (see ch. 75) and the Gurdwara Guru Nanak Parkash Sikh Temple (see ch. 42), making for an interesting faith walk within a compact area.

Designed by the architect Kazimierz Kuzminski, the St Stanislaus Kostka church is a rectangular building of brown and red brick, and is styled in a mid-20th-century fashion with an entrance porch, nave and chancel. Ornate iron gates stand at its entrance, and the church tower, which wasn't constructed until some years later in 1974, is very eye-catching – it's tiled white, with a number of black crosses as detailing. At its summit is a metal steeple topped with a cross. Masses are held in Polish.

There's also a Polish Community Centre on the premises, which over the years has hosted social meetings, games and sports activities such as chess, table tennis and billiards. There's also a Polish Saturday school to educate young children in Polish language and culture.

**Address** Springfield Road, CV1 4GR | **Getting there** 7-minute ride on the 20 bus from Pool Meadow station | **Hours** Unrestricted | **Tip** Cash's Park, named after J&J Cash, a major 19th-century Coventry firm known for its woven products and ribbon-making, is a green oasis beside the canal that's just a 5-minute walk away.

# 82 Starley Road Mural

*Pictorial commemoration of residents' victory*

More than 40 years have elapsed since Starley Road was subject to a campaign by residents protesting at plans for redevelopment. Starley Road is named after James Starley, one of Coventry's most famous sons, acknowledged as the father of the bicycle industry. This row of late-Victorian terraced houses is located just inside the western curve of Coventry's central ring road, and best-known for the eye-catching mural linked to this campaign.

Back in the 1970s, as the post-war city centre of car parks and shopping precincts had spread outwards, there was talk of demolishing Starley Road, the only remaining inner-city street. At the time, many of the 60 terraced houses on the road had fallen into disrepair and were boarded up.

In 1977, the city council took the decision to demolish the buildings, and replace them with a tower block; but the planners hadn't reckoned on the strength of feeling among the remaining Starley Road residents. Around half a dozen families mobilised, and launched a campaign to force the city's council to sit up and listen to their objections to its plans. A masterstroke was the painting of a huge mural the full height of a terraced house at the end of the street, in view of passing traffic on the busy ring road. The painting depicted a tower block struck through with the words, 'Starley Road – Save It!' As a result of the campaign, plans to demolish the street were shelved.

The residents went on to form the Starley Housing Cooperative, taking group ownership of the properties – previously a mix of council houses and privately-owned homes – which gave access to government loans for repairs, or to convert buildings into flats for rental to those in need. The mural has since been repainted to show the residents in cheerful solidarity in celebration of their success, alongside the words, *We Saved It!*

Address Starley Road CV1 3JU | Getting there 9-minute walk from Coventry railway station | Hours Unrestricted | Tip Just a 5-minute walk from Starley Road, visitors can enjoy a fascinating series of stylised carvings by the artist John Skelton. They are located on the concrete colonnades of the Co-operative building, formerly a Co-op store built in the 1950s, more recently converted into upmarket flats.

# 83 Teezers Cocktail Bar

*Crazy golf for grown-ups with a 1980s'*
*and 1990s' twist*

Opened in 2018, Teezers is a cocktail bar featuring an 18-hole indoor crazy golf course with a twist. Built inside the home of a former nightclub known as Club M, Teezers is split over two levels: downstairs is a bar that serves good street food such as burgers and hot dogs along with a range of drinks, while upstairs hosts a crazy golf course, where colourful Clubhouse cocktails and other regular drinks are delivered by waiters, along with a selection of retro sweets. There are also several mini-bars around the perimeter of the course.

The crazy golf course is fabulously colourful and creative – forget the miniature golf courses you might have experienced as a kid: this takes crazy golf to a new level. For starters, it's got a retro-themed focus on iconic imagery from the 1980s and 1990s, and a variety of distinctive holes designed around well-known TV shows, movies, celebrities or games from the era.

Hole themes include the *Jaws* movie, featuring a shark's head that rises from the ground, *Jurassic Park*, with a large T-Rex head, there's the *Bullseye* TV gameshow, including Bully, *Cool Runnings*, that has a bobsled, *Home Alone*, and *Only Fools and Horses*, featuring a replica of the show's distinctive bright yellow Reliant Robin car. A *Friends*-themed hole has a sofa, backdrop of New York city and Central Perk signage, while an *Italian Job* hole features red, white and blue Mini cars. There's also a Tetris-themed hole, and one that replicates the cycling scenes from *ET*. There's also a celebration of Mancunian rockers Oasis, and even a pick 'n' mix store to navigate with your putts. It all adds up to countless opportunities for fun selfies and group pictures to post on social media. Teezers is a venue for over-18s that does a great job of putting a bit of fun, a dash of flair, and some real imagination into Coventry's city centre nightlife experience.

**Address** 2 Hertford Place, CV1 3JZ, +44 (0)24 7655 0884, www.teezersgolf.co.uk | Getting there 8-minute walk around the edge of the ring road from Coventry railway station, or an 8-minute ride on 6, 9 or 10A bus from Pool Meadow station | Hours Mon–Fri 4–10pm, Sat & Sun midday–10pm | Tip Diagonally opposite Teezers, on the other side of the ring road, is the Planet Ice skating rink. It's also home to ice hockey team Coventry Blaze.

# 84 The Acorn Art Controversy
*John and Yoko visit Coventry*

June to August 1968 saw Coventry Cathedral host the Exhibition of British Sculpture, with work on show from artists such as Henry Moore and Barbara Hepworth. Yoko Ono was also keen to be involved with the exhibition, so at short notice the organisers invited her, along with partner John Lennon, to a public event.

So on 15 June, 1968 the couple travelled to Coventry in Lennon's white Rolls-Royce, and they created a conceptual sculpture in which two acorns were planted facing east and west in the Cathedral grounds, symbolising peace. Two halves of a bench would be brought together and the trees would grow upward through the space where the benches met. This took place in what is known today as the Unity Garden. Images from the event show Lennon digging the hole for the acorns, then sitting with Ono on a white, wrought-iron bench, with the Chapel of Unity visible behind them. A plaque was fixed to the seat, which read: *Yoko by John, John by Yoko*. The artwork lasted just a few short days, however.

The acorns were reportedly dug up and stolen, along with the plaque. The bench was also moved, which upset the couple, who had the seating retrieved. It wasn't until 2005, nearly 40 years later, that Yoko Ono returned to the city and planted two Japanese oak trees in Coventry Cathedral's Unity Garden. This act completed that original piece, celebrated the work she and Lennon had undertaken through the years to spread the message of peace, and also recognised Coventry's own commitment to peace and reconciliation. A replica of the white bench was produced for the ceremony, and is now part of a dedicated display to the Acorn Peace controversy in the Coventry Music Museum (see ch. 24). There are now plans for a re-landscaped Unity Garden to include a bench around a tree in the lawn, acknowledging this significant event in the city's cultural history.

Address Unity Lawn, Coventry Cathedral, CV1 5RN | Getting there 12-minute walk from Coventry railway station | Hours Unrestricted | Tip While you're at the cathedral, be sure to check out the West Entrance Screen to the new cathedral, which was engraved by New Zealand-born artist, John Hutton.

# 85__The Albany Theatre
*Fabulous art deco venue and community hub*

The Albany Theatre is a beautifully detailed art deco building just outside the ring road to the west of the city. Originally built as a lecture theatre as part of Coventry Technical College, it opened in 1935, and was used through the war years to entertain the public. After the war, it became home to the Midland Theatre Company, which went on to become the repertory company at the Belgrade, and was a hub for community performances, arts societies and dance companies.

When the college ran into financial troubles in the early 1990s, the theatre was threatened with conversion into computer suites. Campaigners persuaded the city's council to protect the theatre with a planning condition that would save the building for use by the community, when the college moved across the city in 2008, and the theatre closed its doors. The site's new owners were required to establish the Butts Theatre Trust, which would operate the re-opened theatre. An army of volunteers carried out repair and restoration work, the theatre was reopened in 2013, and soon employing people once more. In 2017, a 25-year lease was signed, with the option of a further 25 years to occupy the existing building.

Today, the Albany Theatre is run as a charity, and as well as the art deco main house theatre, is home to a new studio space that seats more than 100. The bar and box office area is set to expand with a café and gallery, while the theatre and studio host a full programme of dance, drama, music and comedy events.

The Albany shares a building with a Travelodge, and the original art deco foyer and stairwells remain in place. The main house features a sea of red upholstered seats, a balcony, and accommodates more than 600 people, with plush red curtains, ornate ceiling windows and period fixtures transporting visitors back to a wonderful golden age of theatre.

Address Albany Road, CV5 6JQ, +44 (0)24 7699 8964, www.albanytheatre.co.uk | Getting there 13-minute walk from Coventry railway station, 7-minute ride on the 10, 14 or 18 bus from Pool Meadow station | Hours See website for shows | Tip The Criterion Theatre, just half a mile away from the Albany, on Berkeley Road South in Earlsdon, opened in 1961, and puts on a handful of shows each year, including classic dramas, comedies and musicals.

# 86 The Brickmakers Arms
*Pretty pub at the edge of green belt country*

The Brickmakers Arms is a delightful little 17th-century pub in the village of Balsall Common, around one and a half miles west of Coventry's city boundary, and just a 200-metre walk from Berkswell train station. Getting to it from Coventry involves a lovely journey, winding through pretty countryside that forms part of the West Midlands green belt, a protected rural space.

The Brickmakers Arms – or 'The Brickies' as it's known by locals – is a Grade II-listed building that takes its name from one of the industries that was once very important to the area, given the abundance of heavy clay in the surrounding Berkswell Parish, which is ideal for brick-making. The building is a two-storey half-timbered construction filled in with red brick. It has diamond pane glass to the entry porch and sash windows on either side, and is always lined with hanging baskets and carefully maintained pot plants, making for a welcoming entrance.

Inside, much of that timber frame remains exposed, and there are three separate bar areas, one of which is laid out around dining tables for those who want to eat. The pub serves a selection of cask ales, draughts, craft beer and fine wines, as well as a varied menu of pub food, plus teas, coffees and homemade cakes, served at lunch time and in the evenings.

Given its location on the edge of wonderful walking countryside, The Brickies welcomes walkers and dogs, and outside is a pretty little beer garden, perfect for a summer visit. It features several traditional pub benches with parasols for shade, plus an interesting multi-coloured wall that gives the space a lift as a backdrop, and makes it feel like a party environment. The pub also offers good accommodation for those who want to explore the area further, with three double rooms and a single room located in the Brickmakers Cottage, which has a separate entrance to the pub itself.

**Address** 307 Station Road, Berkswell, CV7 7EG, +44 (0)1676 533890, www.thebrickmakersberkswell.com | **Getting there** Walk of a couple of minutes from Berkswell railway station | **Hours** Daily midday–11pm | **Tip** Also on Coventry's western boundary, around two miles from the Brickies, TeamSport Indoor Karting is a 500-metre indoor track on multiple levels that's great fun for all the family.

# 87 — The Broomfield Tavern
*Traditional pub specialising in real ale*

The Broomfield Tavern – a Victorian pub known to locals as the Broomy – isn't much to look at from the outside. With metal beer kegs surrounding small tables and doubling as seating for those who want to drink al fresco, it could perhaps do with a lick of paint – but don't let its appearance put you off.

The Broomfield Tavern is a genuine free house, a Spon End community-style pub with a small bar that's home to great hand-pumped beer, which often features unusual choices that are otherwise hard to find in Coventry. Its two regular beers are Church End Fallen Angel, and the Froth Blowers Brewing Co's Piffle Snonker. The other ales it serves, through up to 10 taps, are just as creatively named, and chalked on a board, giving the establishment a permanent beer-festival feel.

The ales the Broomy serves are sourced from a wide range of breweries across the country. Bottled beers are sourced from the continent, while real ciders and perries have always been a hit with the pub's regular clientele. This approach makes the Broomfield Tavern a hit with Campaign for Real Ale (CAMRA) fans, and it is deservedly a regular fixture in the consumer organisation's listings guides and regional awards. Indeed, it was most recently named CAMRA's Coventry Pub of the Year and Cider Pub of the Year 2020. On Friday nights the pub plays host to music sessions, often featuring well-known local musicians, with further sessions on a Monday and Thursday. It has friendly and welcoming staff, and an open fire that adds to the cosy feel of the pub's interior. Pub grub isn't available, however.

Located just around the corner from Coventry Rugby Club, the Broomfield Tavern is more than 150 years old, and remains a favourite meeting place for a number of local interest groups, plus a hit with dog owners thanks to the open green space of the park next door.

Address 14–16 Broomfield Place, CV5 6GY, +44 (0)24 7663 0969 | Getting there Walk just under a mile from Coventry railway station, or a 10-minute ride on the 18 bus from Pool Meadow station | Hours Thu–Sun midday–midnight, Mon–Wed 4pm–midnight | Tip While Coventry City football club play their home games outside the city at the time of writing, Coventry United football club – in the ninth tier of English football – play next door at the Butts Park Arena.

# 88 __ The Bucket Residence

*Home to one of British comedy's best-loved stars*

*Keeping up Appearances* was a sitcom by Roy Clarke that aired on BBC1 from 1990 to 1995. Filmed at a number of locations in Coventry and Warwickshire, it was a huge success both at home and abroad. The star of the show was the would-be social climber and snob, Hyacinth Bucket, played by Patricia Routledge. One of the running jokes through the series was that she insisted people pronounce her surname *Bouquet*. Meanwhile, long-suffering husband Richard, played by Clive Swift, usually bore the brunt of her pompous pronouncements and awful behaviour.

'The Bouquet Residence, the lady of the house speaking,' was how Hyacinth frequently answered the phone, and the property itself – the exterior of which appears regularly in the series – is a pretty bungalow, a private home, in the Binley Woods area of Coventry. This was the base from which Hyacinth conducted her campaigns in an attempt to raise her social standing, both in her own eyes, and those of her affluent neighbours. Meanwhile, she attempted to distance herself from her extended lower-class family, and the reality of her humble upbringing. The plot of each episode broadly revolved around Hyacinth desperately trying to protect her own social standing and veneer of refinement from social humiliation. Her sisters Daisy and Rose, and Daisy's husband Onslow, regularly appeared at inconvenient moments to thwart her efforts. The exterior shots of the small terraced house where Daisy and Onslow lived in the show were also filmed in Coventry, at 3 Mitchell Close in Stoke Aldermoor.

In the show's opening sequence Hyacinth writes an invitation to one of her trademark exclusive candlelight suppers, and lists her address as Waney Edge, Blossom Avenue in the fictional Fuddleton. *Keeping up Appearances* still charts high in polls of the best British sitcoms of all time, and is one of the BBC's most exported TV programmes.

Address 117 Heather Road, CV3 2BD | Getting there 20-minute ride on the 86 bus from Pool Meadow station | Hours Unrestricted, and not open to the public. | Tip There's a scheduled monument – a moated site – at Ernesford Grange on Princethorpe Way in Binley. Excavations in 1971 revealed the site once had a sandstone building at its centre, and was once part of the Coombe Abbey estate.

# 89 The Coventry Carol

*Launchpad of a hugely popular Christmas tune*

Originally performed on the steps of Coventry's old cathedral, the Coventry Carol is regularly cited today as one of the country's most popular carols, and has been recorded by performers such as Sting, Annie Lennox, Alison Moyet, Charlotte Church, Christine McVie of Fleetwood Mac, and even John Denver.

The carol was originally performed in the 16th century as part of a mystery play – that is, a medieval drama based on the Bible – known as *The Pageant of the Sherman and Tailors*. The carol itself refers to the grisly slaughter of the innocents, a story from chapter two in the Gospel of Matthew, in which Herod ordered all males under two years old in Bethlehem to be killed. In the play, the song is a haunting lullaby sung by the mothers of the doomed children, but is sung today by children throughout the city's schools at Christmas time.

The author of the lyrics is unknown, but the oldest known text was written in 1534 by Robert Croo, who managed the Coventry guild pageants. It became widely known, and repurposed as a Christmas carol, only after it featured in the BBC's Empire broadcast on Christmas Day in 1940, after the Coventry Blitz. On that day, Coventry cathedral's Provost Howard spoke of how the enemy had rained devastating fire and destruction on the city from the sky, but he pledged Coventrians were trying hard to banish all thoughts of revenge and instead to make a kinder, simpler world in the days ahead. Around him, in the ruins of the cathedral, were the few people he could muster from the choir to sing the ancient Coventry Carol.

The audio file of this sermon, and the choir's rendition of the carol, is widely available online, and remains an incredibly powerful and moving broadcast. The lyrics are a lament to what has been lost, and it has become both an enduring Christmas carol, and one of Coventry's best-known musical exports.

**Address** Priory Street, CV1 5FB | **Getting there** Coventry's Pool Meadow bus station is less than 200 metres away | **Hours** Unrestricted | **Tip** See the Cross of Nails in the New Cathedral, which was made of three nails from the roof of the Old Cathedral, and now sits in the centre of the altar cross.

# 90 The Elephant Mast
### Coventry's traditional city centre meeting point

The Elephant Mast, more formally known as the Broadgate Standard, was erected in 1948. It's a Grade II-listed statue of an Elephant and Castle perched atop a 15-metre pole in the upper precinct, overlooking Broadgate.

Conceived as a symbol of the spirit of Coventry following the World War II bombings, sections were funded by donations from various industrial firms within the city. The mast, which is built within an octagonal section, was made by British Press Panel, and supplied by Sir W. G. Armstrong Whitworth Aircraft Company. The iconic elephant and castle were supplied by Motor Panels, the aluminium gilding by John Astley and Sons, the flags – the yard arms were designed to fly flags originally – by Holbrooks.

The elephant is at the heart of the city's coat of arms and may have been chosen for its religious symbolism and strength. It's depicted carrying Coventry's castle with three domed turrets, flanked on either side by a black eagle and a phoenix rising from the flames, with a wild cat crest. It's located between Broadgate House and what was formerly the Hotel Leofric, which were part of City Architect Sir Donald Gibson's masterplan to modernise the city, drawn up in 1941, and for Coventrians, 'underneath the elephant' is a well-known and commonly agreed meeting point. The elephant has gazed down on a changing Broadgate over the years, from back when the area was first laid out as a tree-lined square, through the years a tent covered the Lady Godiva statue, to its open pedestrianised plan today.

It took a team of firemen, and a fully extended high ladder, to help install the elephant and castle, gleaming and new, in place. The standard was originally painted and the elephant covered in gold leaf, but weathering over the years means this colourful detailing is no longer visible to pedestrians looking up from ground level in Broadgate.

Address Broadgate, CV1 1NE | Getting there 15-minute walk from Coventry railway station, 5-minute walk from Pool Meadow bus station | Hours Unrestricted | Tip From Peeping Tom to Lady Godiva, a cantilevered clock to the four patron saints of the British Isles, all the eye-catching sculptures that adorn Coventry's Council House were produced by Henry Wilson, and are just a 3-minutes' walk from from the Elephant Mast.

# The Glass Bridge
*Spiral walkway that'll put a spring in your step*

This Glass Bridge, located in Millennium Place, was opened in 2004, and is a fine example of architecture as art. The brainchild of London architect Sir Richard MacCormac, the bridge was produced as part of the Phoenix Initiative – the council's Millennium scheme – that regenerated a neglected area of Coventry. The bridge begins as a long ramp beside the Motor Museum, before its steel tubular spine, overlaid with a deck for pedestrians, coils and winds snake-like up and over Lady Herbert's Garden and the medieval city wall, before setting down again in the garden of International Friendship. Pairs of blue, curved glass panels that look like fins, and which are engraved with designs by the artist Alexander Beleschenko, flank the balustrades every few feet on either side, lending the bridge its name.

The bridge is 130 metres in length, and supported by steel columns, although the eye-catching spiral that winds from Millennium Place at the western end is unsupported. Dampers inside the steel tubular spine here maintain some level of stability, but pedestrians definitely feel an extra spring in their step as they traverse the bridge!

Visually, the bridge is at its best at night: the deck system has grilles designed to allow rainwater to run off, and lighting installed beneath results in a strip-like effect as the deck is illuminated from the underside. The blue glass fins reflect and scatter this light, creating a beautiful display. In truth, the footbridge isn't carrying out a genuinely useful function – walking at ground level around the walled Lady Herbert's Garden will get you from one end to the other in just about the same amount of time. Furthermore, it's rarely busy – most Coventrians take the low road, which is a shame because the views over the gardens give a different perspective on this ancient part of the city.

Address Millennium Place, Hales Street, CV1 1JD | Getting there Coventry's main bus station, Pool Meadow, is adjacent | Hours Unrestricted | Tip Walk 5 minutes along Corporation Street and Upper Well Street to see the *Two Sides of a Woman* sculpture. Although somewhat concealed by bushes, this Helaine Blumenfeld artwork is definitely worth seeking out.

# 92 The Golden Cross

*One of Cov's oldest pubs is an architectural gem*

The Golden Cross is a much-loved pub within a Grade II-listed Tudor building, and features coloured-glass leaded windows of the Northampton Brewery Company. Believed to have been constructed in 1583, during the reign of Queen Elizabeth I, it was first established as a public house in 1661. The pub is in the middle of Coventry's splendid medieval centre, the Cathedral Quarter, among a warren of cobbled streets. It stands alongside other survivors of the World War II bombing raids, such as the Holy Trinity Church, St Mary's Guild Hall, and the old Cathedral of St Michael.

The pub has undergone countless restorations over the years, but the overall structure is unchanged. The building features an exposed timber-frame construction, and includes a 'dragon beam' architectural design. This complex building technique allows the upper floors to be 'jettied' – that is to project out beyond the floors below, even at the corners.

The building is thought to stand on what was previously the mint, from the time when Coventry was given the right to mint coins by Edward IV in the 15th century. This monetary heritage, coupled with the pub's proximity to the nearby Coventry Cross, a market cross common to medieval English market towns, is believed to be the source of the pub's name.

The Golden Cross isn't a modern sports pub, so while sports lovers may be disappointed that the big matches and events aren't broadcast here, it means the atmosphere is pleasant but never rowdy. A wide range of real ales, gins and decent pub grub are on offer, and live music lovers should visit the pub on a Saturday, when there are regular gigs in the upstairs room. In the past the pub has hosted famed Coventry bands such as The Specials, The Primitives and The Selecter. It's also been a favourite boozer for some of the city's most famous inhabitants, including the poet Philip Larkin.

Address 8 Hay Lane, CV1 5RF, +44 (0)24 7655 1855, www.thegoldencrosscoventry.co.uk |
Getting there 12-minute walk from Coventry railway station | Hours Food served Mon–Sat
midday–9pm, Sun midday–5pm | Tip The Old Windmill on Spon Street is another city
centre pub that's Grade II listed, and is thought to date from the 15th century. It even
features a priest hole in the fireplace.

# 93 The Green-Roofed House

*Distinctive 1950s' architectural landmark*

On the A45, also known as the Fletchamstead Highway, stands a distinctive white-walled house that features a roof tiled in eye-catching shades of sea-green clay tiles. The A45 is a major road running east to west and bisecting the south side of Coventry, and the house stands at a busy junction, where the A-road meets the Kenilworth Road heading south from the city centre. As a result, it's a familiar site to the commuters who sit in traffic there, no doubt reflecting on this interesting structure.

The house was built in 1956 by Jean and William Tooth, who were living nearby when they saw the land for sale. Accountant William bought the three-quarters of an acre plot for £1,100, while the building cost a further £7,000. They named the house Green Roofs, and when new the house was reportedly very fashionable and stylish inside, in addition to its attention-grabbing roof. It had Muhuhu Wood parquet floors, and there was also a tennis court in the garden. It was the owners' intention that it should remain fashionable for at least 20 years. Their son, Nicholas, buried a time capsule beneath it, stuffed with newspaper clippings and coins.

The green, interlocking clay roofing tiles were sourced from a company called Langley's in London. Jean's brother-in-law Ralph worked at Langley's as chief accountant, and according to her grand-daughter they got the sea green tiles at a bargain price, in return for allowing the home to be used for photographic purposes to appear in the tile supplier's advertising literature.

In the 1970s the house was sold to the Ministry of the Environment in preparation for a flyover that never came to pass, and it was later owned by nearby Warwick University and operated as student accommodation. More than 60 years after its construction, the original clay green tiles remain today, and are something of a quirky landmark within the city. Today, it's a private residence.

Address Fletchamstead Highway, CV4 7AR | Getting there 15-minute ride on the 12X bus from Pool Meadow station | Hours Unrestricted | Tip If quirky architecture's your thing, the Houses for Visiting Mathematicians, part of Warwick University, are a short walk up Gibbet Hill Road.

# 94 The Greyhound Inn

*A great rest stop on a canal walk or cycle ride*

A traditional venue in a lovely location beside Coventry Canal's junction with the Oxford Canal, the Greyhound Inn is a pub that dates from the early 1800s. These former canal cottages make a great destination for a good meal and a pint at the end of the Coventry Canal conservation area and art trail walk (see ch. 16). The five and a half mile tow path is also a hit with cyclists, as part of Sustrans' National Cycle Route Number 52.

Even though it's quite close to the M6 as it passes to the north of Coventry, the Greyhound's location is a calm oasis. The view of the canal from the front of the pub, where benches and tables deck the tow path, is stunning. The canal is normally lined with narrowboats, and a gorgeous and beautifully preserved cast iron bridge spans the junction of the canals, which is prominently marked with the details of its manufacture: *Britannia Foundry Derby 1837*. With pretty cottages and houses on the opposite bank, it's a view that brings people back time and time again.

Inside, the inn is cosy and dark, with low ceilings and exposed timber beams. The odd hollowed-out wooden keg converted into seating is a nice touch, and there's plenty of wood panelling, a wood burner, countless brass ornaments and trinkets to give this pub the patina of age. There are also plenty of fun adverts and banners from years gone by, plus plenty more pub paraphernalia and knick-knacks to hold visitors' attention.

It's been voted 'best pub in Coventry and Warwickshire' on four separate occasions, and is a previous winner of the Campaign for Real Ale's Best Pub in Coventry. Its food is more at the gastro end of pub grub than the cheap and cheerful, with quality pies and the roast beef recommended. There's also a good selection of cask ales on tap, plus draught beer, including regular guest beers and cider, while out back there's a decent beer garden to be enjoyed.

Address Sutton Stop, Hawkesbury Junction, CV6 6DF, +44 (0)24 7636 3046, www.thegreyhoundlongford.co.uk | Getting there 30-minute ride on the 6A bus from Pool Meadow station | Hours Daily midday–11pm | Tip The Greyhound is popular for fans of Wasps Rugby Club, with the Ricoh Arena a little over a mile away. While visiting the stadium for a match, also check out the wall of fame at the Ricoh – bricks that carry the names of supporters who helped build a new home for Coventry's Sky Blues football team.

# 95_ The Herbert

*Spectacular gallery that's a work of art in itself*

The Herbert – or to give it its full name, The Herbert Art Gallery & Museum – is an interactive museum, art gallery, media studio and home to the creative arts in Coventry. It's named after Sir Alfred Herbert, the Coventry industrialist and philanthropist, who donated £100,000 and laid the foundation stone of the building in 1954. Herbert died at the age of 90, before the building could open to the public in 1960.

Inside, The Herbert's permanent collections include sculptures, paintings by old masters and more modern artworks, as well as collections relating to the city's history as a centre for ribbon and watchmaking. Recent years have seen temporary exhibitions, such as a project to show children what life as an evacuee would have been like in the 1940s, along with eye-catching displays of pop art, the work of Grayson Perry, local artist George Shaw, and an exhibition on the history of video games. Beneath it lies a medieval undercroft, which belonged to a wealthy cloth merchant, and is the subject of special open days. Also drop in at Alfred's, the in-house café, for a range of coffees, sandwiches, cakes and locally brewed beers.

The Herbert recently received a shot in the arm when more than £15 million was spent on a complete refurbishment, which concluded in 2008. The jewel in the crown of this renovation was the new 500-square-metre roof, a grid of wood and glass that curves and rolls like a wave, creating a fabulous, high-ceilinged atrium. This created an entrance from Bayley Lane that faces the Cathedral. The roof line stops a few metres short of a row of rusted-steel panels erected along the edge of Bayley Lane, which signify the location of medieval building plots. The Herbert is now one of the most popular free tourist attractions in the West Midlands, seeing around 300,000 visitors per year, compared to 80,000 before its redevelopment.

Address Jordan Well, CV1 5QP, +44 (0)24 7623 7521, www.theherbert.org | **Getting there** Short walk along Priory Street past the cathedral from Pool Meadow bus station | **Hours** Mon–Sat 10am–4pm, Sun midday–4pm | **Tip** Frederick McWilliam's *Elisabeth Frink* statue – a sculpture of the woman who created the eagle lectern in Coventry Cathedral – stands just outside The Herbert, as one of its finer exterior pieces.

# 96 The Kasbah

*A nightclub and venue for over a century*

The Kasbah is a live music venue and nightclub with a history stretching back more than 100 years, making it one of Coventry's best-loved and most enduring venues. The statuesque building on Primrose Hill Street in the Hillfields area started out as a movie house – the Globe Picture Theatre – back in 1914. It continued to screen movies until its closure in 1956, re-opening the following year as the Majestic Ballroom, hosting big bands, orchestras and modern dance. In 1962 it was taken over by the Mecca organisation, and reopened as the Orchid Ballroom under the stewardship of Larry Page. Page had toured as a pop star in his own right, with Cliff Richard, and later went on to manage The Troggs and The Kinks, as well as setting up his own record label. The dance hall even spawned a teenage girl band – The Orchids – who Page discovered in a talent contest at the venue.

The Orchid Ballroom closed in the late 1960s and the building fell into disuse, before being resurrected as a music venue by local lad Jon Gaunt. Gaunt and his co-operative theatre company won funding from West Midlands Arts and the Arts Council of Britain, and used it to buy and renovate the hall, reopening it as the Tic Toc Club in 1990. Britpop bands such as Blur and Ocean Colour Scene, and American rockers Pixies, were among the big names to play at the venue. Gaunt went on to become an award-winning and controversial radio presenter and newspaper columnist.

The venue changed hands and reopened in 1995 as the Colosseum, or 'the Colly', hosting bands such as The Libertines, Arctic Monkeys and Keane, as well as popular club nights. Finally, after a 12-year run, it relaunched in 2007 as the Kasbah, which it remains today. In its latest form, the venue is particularly popular with Coventry's student population, and continues to host live bands such as La Roux and Noah and the Whale.

**Address** Primrose Hill Street, CV1 5LY, www.kasbahnightclub.com | Getting there
7-minute walk from Pool Meadow bus station | Hours Mon 10pm–5am, Fri 10pm–4am,
Sat 9pm–4am | Tip Half a mile away, a blue plaque next to a playground in Signet
Square bears the words *Site of Highfield Road Stadium, home of Coventry City Football Club
1899–2005* marking the former location of the ground used by the 1987 FA Cup winners.

# 97___The Public Bench

*Artwork celebrating friendships and encounters*

The Public Bench is an artwork located in Coventry's Millennium Place. It bears pairs of names engraved into more than 4,000 red enamel plaques, which are fixed to a 45-metre curved wall above a wooden bench. This public artwork is the brainchild of Jochen Gerz, a German conceptual artist who is known for producing work that focuses on history, memory and public spaces.

The bench was installed in 2004 as part of the Phoenix Initiative – a lottery-funded scheme to overhaul the city centre between Broadgate and the Transport Museum. The artwork seeks to capture and commemorate friendships, secret relationships and memorable encounters. The visitor centre in Priory Place received hundreds of forms from Coventrians and visitors to the city who wanted to record names on the artwork's plaques. The local evening newspaper, the *Coventry Telegraph*, played its part, featuring stories of people who had taken plaques, and running a scheme in which its readership collected tokens from the newspaper in order to secure a plaque of their own. Alongside their own name, people could select the names of loved ones, friends, people they admired but had never met, fictional characters, or names from legend – any name they desired.

The result is an engaging visual treat that still attracts and intrigues visitors more than 15 years after the artwork's installation. It's easy to spend a long time reading the various inscriptions and wondering about the people depicted. Although the plaques carry only a date and names, they still manage to convey a wealth of emotions, from recollection to loss and love. They are all intensely personal to the individuals concerned, and visiting and absorbing the human relationships of those featured is a moving and worthwhile experience. As Gerz himself said: 'In order to understand each couple's inscription more fully, one has to contribute oneself.'

**Address** Millennium Place, Hales Street, CV1 1JD | **Getting there** Coventry's main bus station, Pool Meadow, is adjacent | **Hours** Unrestricted | **Tip** A second Gerz artwork, *The Future Monument* is also located in Millennium Place. 6,000 participants identified enemy countries from the past, and those most commonly mentioned – today celebrated as friends – are engraved on plaques surrounding a glass obelisk that's nearly 5 metres high.

# 98 The Sherbourne Viaduct
*Awesome engineering from railways' golden age*

Locals refer to it as the seven arches, but the viaduct carrying trains over Coventry's River Sherbourne is a remarkable piece of architecture. At the time of writing the viaduct is set to become an impressive and widely admired landmark once more, as part of the planned Charterhouse Heritage Park – one of the projects undertaken by the Historic Coventry Trust, a charity launched in 2015 to champion heritage at risk in Coventry.

The Charterhouse Heritage Park will surround the historic Charterhouse – a Grade I-listed former Carthusian monastery – as an eco-friendly corridor that brings wildlife and the countryside right into the city. As part of the project, the overgrown banks of the River Sherbourne will be restored to their natural state, and a new wetland area created to lead visitors to Sherbourne Viaduct.

The viaduct consists of seven tall, elegant arches – a large central arch, with three smaller arches to either side – and is Grade II-listed. It still carries London to Birmingham trains, via Rugby and Coventry, across the river today. It was originally built as part of Robert Stephenson's railway line connecting Birmingham and London, and has been described as the world's first major inter-city railway. Its construction was finally completed in 1838, at the height of the Industrial Revolution.

Sadly, this historic treasure is hidden from view by trees and overgrown shrubbery, and is adorned with a fair amount of colourful graffiti, but its elegant arches are much-loved by local dog walkers and ramblers. It's worth getting a little mud on your shoes to experience a truly spectacular piece of engineering, and an early example of a viaduct dating from Britain's golden age of railway development. Follow the Sherbourne on foot eastwards across the playing fields by the Charterhouse and Blue Coat School, and you'll soon find yourself under its arches.

**Address** Just east of the A414, behind Bar Road, CV3 4AN | **Getting there** 20-minute
ride on the X18 bus from Pool Meadow station, then walk just under half a mile | **Hours**
Unrestricted | **Tip** For football fans, George Singer, founder of the Singer Cycle Company,
and whose works' football team, Singer FC, later evolved into Coventry City FC, is buried
in the nearby London Road Cemetery.

# 99 The Village Cross

*Meriden's questionable claim as centre of England*

On a pretty little village green in Meriden, a couple of miles outside Coventry's north-west boundary, is a Grade II-listed medieval
sandstone monument. Mounted on an octagonal plinth with three
worn steps supporting the stone base, it's clearly maintained with
civic pride.

The cross is bordered by seasonal plants, a small fence and a
well-maintained plaque dating from 1951, which reads: *This ancient
wayside cross has stood in the village for some 500 years and by tradition it marks the centre of England. The cross was rebuilt on this site
when the green was improved in celebration of the Festival of Britain.*
Strictly speaking, though, it's no longer a cross – more of a pillar –
as time and the British elements have eroded its substance over the
centuries.

Meriden is historically part of Warwickshire, and remains in the
ecclesiastical parish of the Diocese of Coventry, in pretty greenbelt
countryside. The cross was originally located in the old centre of the
village, but was moved to the village green in 1822, and again to its
current position on the village green in 1952. Meriden is a lovely,
low-key village, that has resisted spoiling its picturesque ambience
with tea shops and amusement arcades to capitalise on its status as
the traditional centre of England. Even the monument itself is unas-
suming, and could easily be missed by unknowing passers-by.

Indeed, Meriden's reluctance to invest in tourism is perhaps well
judged, as analysis conducted by the Ordnance Survey in 2002, using
modern GPS satellites, calculated the exact centre of England to be
some 11 miles north of Meriden, in a field at Lindley Hall Farm
in Fenny Drayton, Leicestershire – that is, the location at which a
three-dimensional model of England would balance on a point. Evi-
dence, if any were needed, that science doesn't carry the romance of
tradition and storytelling.

Address The Green, Meriden, CV7 7LN | Getting there 25-minute ride on the X20 or X1 bus from Pool Meadow station to Meriden green | Hours Unrestricted | Tip The Village Cross isn't the only, or even the most eye-catching monument on Meriden's village green: just 50 yards away is the much more prominent, nine-metre-tall National Cyclists memorial, dedicated to the cyclists who died in World War I.

# 100 Three Spires View
### *A clear perspective on the famous trinity*

Coventry is known as the City of Three Spires, for its trinity of medieval cathedral and church spires. Huge growth of Coventry and Warwick universities in recent years, however, has prompted construction of a glut of boldly-coloured high-rise blocks to accommodate tens of thousands of additional students. As a result, it's become difficult to see the city's historic three spires from a single viewpoint.

The spires comprise Holy Trinity, the old cathedral, and Christchurch, all of which escaped the World War II bombings unscathed. Holy Trinity Church dates from the 12th century, and is the only medieval church in the city that is still complete, with a spire standing at 72 metres. St Michael's Church, dating from the 14th century, became a cathedral in 1918, and while much of this building was destroyed in the bombing, the 90-metre tower remains Coventry's tallest structure.

Then there's Christchurch, previously known as Greyfriars, which dates from the 14th century, and stands 61 metres tall. Christchurch's tower and spire survived Henry VIII's dissolution of the monasteries, and while the church was rebuilt in the 19th century, only the resilient tower and spire survived the 1941 bombing. Until recently a bar, at time of writing it is unoccupied.

With much of the high-rise student accommodation built to the north and east of the city centre, the best place to see the three spires from street level is to the south west, beyond the ring road. A footbridge spans the railway line between the Central Six shopping complex and the pretty Spencer Park, lined by an avenue of trees. The three spires – and so the romantic and historic Coventry skyline of centuries – can be seen aligned in tight formation from Burger King at Central Six, and also along the footbridge and in the park. They can be glimpsed from ground level in a handful of other locations, but only by peeking between other buildings.

Address Central Six, Warwick Road, CV3 6TA | Getting there 5-minute walk west from Coventry railway station | Hours Unrestricted | Tip Less than half a mile away from Spencer Park is Earlsdon Library, a locally listed building, which dates back to 1912, when it was endowed by multi-millionaire steel magnate Andrew Carnegie, one of the richest men of his time.

# 101 Thrust SSC

*Jet-powered car that broke the sound barrier*

Thrust SCC is one of the prize exhibits in the Coventry Transport Museum. It's the car in which Wing Commander Andy D. Green OBE set the world land speed record on 15 October, 1997. He became the first person to break the sound barrier on land by reaching the speed of 763.035 miles per hour in the car. The record speed was achieved as an average of two runs over a measured mile on the dry lake at Black Rock Desert in Nevada. It's a milestone that stands to this day.

Richard Noble, who previously held the world land speed record since 1983, developed the jet-engined Thrust SSC – or Thrust Super Sonic Car – with the help of missile designer Ron Ayers, seeking to extend the record even further. They used computational fluid dynamics and wind tunnel testing to settle on the body shape, which sees the two giant engines located on either side of the cockpit, and a nose cone that tapers to a point like a jet fighter aircraft. The suspension is active, adjusting to minimise lift and wheel drag.

Noble decided not to drive the car himself for this record attempt, which is where Andy Green came in. After obtaining a first class honours degree in mathematics at Oxford University, Green became an RAF fighter pilot, flying F4 Phantom and Tornado F3 aircraft. Green saw off more than 30 competitors for the honour of being Thrust SSC's driver, and played an active role in developing the cockpit, making it look and feel like those of the jet fighters he was used to flying. The rear-wheel-drive car is 16.5 metres long, 3.7 metres wide, and weighs 10.5 tons. It's powered by two Rolls-Royce Spey 202 engines – the type used in the Phantom II jet Green was experienced in flying – generating 10 tons of thrust each. Getting this close to Thrust SSC, it's possible to see where the paint was stripped from the vehicle by the blast generated from its engines as it made its record-breaking runs.

Address Millennium Place, Hales Street, CV1 1JD, +44 (0)24 7623 4270, www.transport-museum.com | Getting there Coventry's main bus station, Pool Meadow, is adjacent | Hours Daily 10am–5pm | Tip The previous record-holding vehicle, Thrust 2, is located near Thrust SSC in the same museum. Plans are underway to build Bloodhound LSR, to be driven again by Andy Green, this time at more than 1,000mph, and you can find more on this in the museum too.

# 102 Tin Music and Arts

*Canal Basin community hub and venue*

The Tin Music and Arts at the Coventry Canal Basin, just north of the ring road, is another of the city's great live music venues. Sadly unable to open for music and other events for most of 2020 due to the COVID-19 pandemic, this intimate venue is located in neighbouring buildings that were former coal vaults, integrated neatly with surviving canal architecture. Today, the imposing coal vault doors have a light wood panel coating, concealing their industrial heritage. In their previous life they would have been a hive of activity in the 18th century, busy with the coal movements that were once an essential part of the basin's activity at this city centre hub. The basin is also the starting point for the five-mile canal towpath and art trail (see ch. 16).

The Tin Music and Arts – formerly known as Taylor John's, itself a mainstay of Coventry's vibrant music scene – took over and refurbished the venue in 2013. It's part of the PRS for Music Foundations Talent Development Partnership Programme, a charitable funder of new music and talent development, which since 2000 has awarded more than £35 million to over 7,300 new music projects. Finance from PRS has supported The Tin's Music Creator Development Project over the last several years.

The Tin's two main rooms have a stage and performance area, plus a bar and seating. Next door is the office and rehearsal space, artist studio and community room. The set up means The Tin Music and Arts plays host to regular live music events with established and international acts, as well as more local, homegrown talent. Sometimes it hosts art exhibitions, other programmes and events, for private hire, or for the local university. In normal circumstances the Tin is also home to artists by day, and is a great venue for arts workshops in its studio, along with many other community activities, such as Tai Chi and Yoga classes.

**Address** Units 1-4, Canal Basin, CV1 4LY, +44 (0)24 7623 0699, www.thetinmusicandarts.org.uk | Getting there BS5 or BS7 bus from Pool Meadow station, then a 3-minute walk, or a 20-minute walk from Coventry railway station via Broadgate and the Burges | Hours See website for events | Tip There's a 2-Tone trail plaque at the Canal Basin: it was here in 1979 where photographers Chalkie Davies and Carol Starr took a set of iconic images that were used as the cover artwork on The Specials' albums.

# 103__ Tom Mann Plaque

*Birthplace of a working-class hero*

Tom Mann, one of the pioneers and best-known names of the international trade union movement, was born in Coventry in 1856, and plaques now adorn the humble, privately owned house in Longford that was his birthplace. Mann helped form what would later become the Transport and General Workers' Union, and campaigned on behalf of workers at home and abroad.

By the age of 10, Mann was at work in a local colliery, where he was a trapper – that is, he would sit underground opening and closing trap doors across the mine. In 1870 the colliery closed, and the Mann family moved to Birmingham, where Tom started an engineering apprenticeship, and began attending political meetings and reading the work of Karl Marx. After his apprenticeship, Mann moved to London where he found work in an engineering shop. He joined the Amalgamated Society of Engineers in 1881, and later the Social Democratic Federation (SDF). In 1889 he was a leading figure in the successful London dock strike and began to gain fame. He was elected President of the Dock, Wharf, Riverside and General Labourers' Union, and became Secretary of the new Independent Labour Party in 1894. In 1897 he helped form the Workers' Union, which eventually became the Transport and General Workers' Union.

As a strong advocate of direct trade union action Mann was imprisoned several times. In 1902, Mann moved to Australia, intent on taking on capitalism to improve workers' rights. He became an organiser for the Australian Labor Party, then founded the Victorian Socialist Party, but grew disillusioned. On his return to the UK, he led the 1911 Liverpool General Transport Strike, and in 1919 became the Secretary of the Amalgamated Society of Engineers, and in 1920 was involved in forming the Communist Party of Great Britain. He published many pamphlets and continued to champion socialism and communism until his death in 1941.

Address 175–177 Grand Road, Longford, CV6 6DD | Getting there 30-minute ride on the 6A bus from Pool Meadow station, followed by a 7-minute walk | Hours Unrestricted | Tip A little over a mile away is the Ricoh Arena, today home to Wasps rugby club. Outside the entrance is a statue of Jimmy Hill, Coventry City Football Club's most heralded manager, who went on to become a much-loved national sports presenter and pundit.

# 104 Twisted Barrel Ale

*Join real ale enthusiasts at this brewery and bar*

This cool micro-brewery and tap house in Coventry's FarGo Village produces a range of craft beers with colourful names, such as the popular session, or lower alcohol, IPA Sine Qua Non (translated as 'without which, nothing') and the oatmeal stout God's Twisted Sister. The artisan vegan venture, founded by Chris Cooper and Ritchie Bosworth, has been running at FarGo since 2015, and expanded into its current premises in 2018, brewing on-site. The shiny brewing equipment – floor-to-ceiling fermenting vessels, kettle, mash tun and liquor tun, all in full few of the tap house and seated bar area, make for a fascinating, industrial backdrop for drinking. Alongside the brewing kit there's fermenting capacity for over 3,000 litres.

Today, there's room for up to 300 people in the tap house, with more than 20 beers available, and as many different bottled beers on offer, sufficient to slake any thirst. There are several beers the team brews throughout the year, a dozen seasonal beers, plus another 40 or so products brewed as one-offs.

As well as the two core beers, Sine Qua Non and God's Twisted Sister, other popular offerings include Beast of a Midlands Mild, Detroit Sour City wheat beer, Lonely Souls Belgian-style blonde and pale ale Pixel Juice. Twisted Barrel also produces porters and stouts.

There's typically a monthly brewery tour, and other regular events include fortnightly open mic and quiz nights. Live bands often play at the Twisted Barrel, and the venue occasionally doubles as an art gallery for private viewings. There are also ad hoc themed days such as a Father Ted day, and an annual beer festival also draws the crowds. Vegan food is served in the tap house, produced by fellow vegan business Dirty Kitch next door. There's also a Home Brew Club of enthusiasts – after all, the business grew out of the home brewing passion of its founders, both local lads.

**Address** Fargo Village, Far Gosford Street, CV1 5ED, www.twistedbarrelale.co.uk | Getting there 25-minute walk from Coventry railway station, or 8 or 13 bus to Far Gosford Street | Hours Vary Wed–Sun, see website for current information on visiting | Tip Less than 100 metres away is FarGo's Escape Live: whether you're pulling off a casino heist or saving the world from Armageddon, this new fashion for escape rooms – in which players have to complete a mission and escape from a room – is a fun outing for all the family.

# 105_ Undercroft Café
*Dramatic eatery beneath historic Guildhall*

The Undercroft café is located beneath the magnificent St Mary's Guildhall, built in the 1340s, and located at the heart of Coventry's historic Cathedral Quarter. Visitors can choose from the lunch menu, take afternoon tea, or just tuck into light snacks, coffee and cake, all of which are served from the same kitchens that have successfully produced grand banquets for visiting royalty and other dignitaries for over 600 years. In 1860, they also became a soup kitchen for starving ribbon weavers and their families, when the trade suffered a collapse and its workers needed support.

The Guildhall is one of the best surviving medieval guildhalls in the country. Originally built for the merchant guild of St Mary, it soon became the headquarters for the city mayor and leaders, and remained that way through the centuries until Coventry's current Council House was built in 1913.

It's still the venue of choice in the city for high-profile conferences and ceremonies. It houses a storied collection of arms, furniture and artworks in its many rooms, but the star turn is the Great Hall, featuring medieval stained-glass windows, a ceiling of carved angels, and a huge tapestry.

The café is closed at time of writing due to building work as part of the Guildhall Transformation Project, which is set to cost around £6 million. This involves stripping away the modern kitchen fittings, such as formica panels and modern stainless steel that were installed to meet modern hygiene standards, to reveal more of the Guildhall's original, hidden medieval features, such as late-Georgian fire grates in the hearths.

The Guildhall, including the Undercroft café, is set to reopen in the summer of 2021. They will be open to the public, and interactive digital guides will bring to life what it would have been like to work in the kitchens in their medieval heyday.

Address Bayley Lane, CV1 5RN, +44 (0)24 7683 3328, www.stmarysguildhall.co.uk/cafe |
Getting there 13-minute walk from Coventry railway station via Hertford Street, or
5-minute walk from Pool Meadow bus station | Hours Mon–Fri 9.30am–4pm | Tip Just
a 2-minute walk away, on the side of The Herbert facing the Ellen Terry building, are two
carved stone murals by Coventry-born artist Walter Ritchie titled *Man's Struggle*, with
nature and with himself.

# 106 Virgins and Castle Pub

*Possible host to historic royal romance*

The famous Virgins and Castle pub is the oldest pub in Kenilworth, a market town just to the south-west of Coventry, that dates back to the 16th century. Back then, it was called the Two Virgins Inn, and reportedly played host to the court of the castle manor – that is, the nearby Kenilworth Castle. In 1563, Queen Elizabeth granted the castle to her lifelong friend, Robert Dudley, whom she also made Earl of Leicester. Although Dudley was already married to Amy Robsart, it was rumoured that he and the Queen were lovers. After his wife's suspicious death in 1560, the scandal surrounding Dudley meant she could never marry him.

Nevertheless, Dudley converted the castle into a lavish and magnificent palace, a venue fit to entertain his queen. And sure enough, he hosted and entertained Elizabeth here on a number of occasions, most famously for 19 days of festivities in 1575. But Queen Elizabeth famously declared she remained a virgin until her death.

In the 18th century the pub was known as the Sign of the Two Virgins, and in the early 19th century it merged with the Castle Tavern, becoming The Virgins and Castle. Today, the pub, which is located at the foot of the sloping Kenilworth High Street, is part of the Leicestershire brewery Everards, perhaps best-known for its Tiger Ale.

The establishment came under new ownership at the start of 2020 when catering and hospitality group Caviar and Chips took on the business. It's an old, traditional pub serving high-quality classic and traditional food to customers at lunch and dinner times. It also offers plant-based menus crafted by chefs who seek the best ingredients from suppliers in and around Warwickshire. It also offers a selection of beers, ales, wines and spirits, plus a temperance bar selection too. The famous Virgins and Castle has a real community spirit, hosting pub quizzes and more.

Address 7 High Street, Kenilworth, Warwickshire, CV8 1LY, +44 (0)1926 853737, www.virginsandcastle.com | Getting there 40-minute ride on the 12X bus from Pool Meadow station, or 13-minute walk from Kenilworth railway station | Hours Daily midday–11pm | Tip Abbey Fields, behind the Virgins and Castle, is a lovely 68-acre park in the undulating valley of Finham Brook, at the centre of which is a child's play area and open air swimming pool.

# 107 — Volgograd Place

*Commemoration to international friendship*

Volgograd Place is a public square in the shadows beneath junction two of the Coventry ring road, which pedestrians walking north from the city centre towards Hillfields and Swanswell Park and Pool pass through. While a little down at heel today, it remains notable for the murals that decorate the stanchions for the flyover, while underfoot the ground is shaped into an undulating concrete garden, or something resembling a rocky moonscape. A pair of hands shake across the ocean, while another pair appear to hold up the ring road flyover.

It's named Volgograd Place to commemorate Coventry's status as the first-ever city to be twinned with another. Back in 1942, when Stalingrad faced devastation during the war, a Coventry women's movement was very vocal in its belief that Britain should provide more help to the Soviet Union, and raised money for the Red Army. In response, thousands of Stalingrad's women signed an album that was sent to Coventry, and in 1944 an official bond of friendship was created when Coventry was partnered with Volgograd – formerly Stalingrad until 1961. Both cities were decimated by war and reached out in mutual support, and in so doing sparked the international twin city movement. Coventry was also twinned with Lidice, Kiel and even Dresden in 1959 – the German city that British Prime Minister Winston Churchill reportedly ordered to be firebombed in World War II, in retaliation for the bombing of Coventry.

The public square was named Volgograd Place in 1972, symbolising the friendship between the two cities in the year that saw Mikhail Zolotaryov, Deputy Mayor of Volgograd, visit Coventry. Although twinning cities has rather fallen out of vogue, Coventry's bond with Volgograd remains. As recently as 2014, Volgograd Children's Orchestra visited and performed in the city to celebrate the original bond of friendship.

Address Hales Street, CV1 5FY | Getting there Pool Meadow bus station is 200 metres along Hales Street | Hours Always open | Tip In St Mark's church, next to the Swanswell Park, is a fabulous mural depicting the ascension, painted in 1963 by Hans Feibusch.

# 108_ War Memorial Monument

*Towering tribute to Coventry's fallen heroes*

At the heart of Coventry's War Memorial Park stands the monument from which it takes its name. In an Art Deco style, it towers to a point almost 90 feet high, with a permanently-lit beacon at its summit to symbolise an eternal light.

The 120-acre park opened in 1921 as a tribute to the more than 2,500 Coventrians who lost their lives fighting in World War I. The War Memorial itself was completed in 1927. Designed by local architect Thomas Francis Tickner, it was built in reinforced concrete clad with Portland stone, with tree-lined footpaths radiating out from the park's centre. The monument has a square footprint on a circular platform, and features five bronze discs that commemorate men of Coventry in the Boer War and World War I who were awarded the Victoria Cross – the highest award of the British honours system – for valour in the presence of the enemy. The monument is sculpted with the dates of the two World Wars, along with the city's coat of arms. Today, both memorial and park are Grade II-listed.

Bronze doors open into an inner chamber – the Chamber of Silence – which originally housed a roll of honour for the fallen, but is now kept in The Herbert and brought into the park each Remembrance Sunday, when the Chamber is accessible to the public. It lists all the servicemen who were killed, and includes those from World War II and subsequent conflicts such as the Gulf War. In 1948, a memorial tree planting campaign began to commemorate local people who have died in conflict. In the visitor centre there's a display called 'The Missing Faces' project, featuring photos of 264 servicemen killed during World War I who have a tree and memorial plaque in the park. The park also features sports fields and children's play equipment. In 1963, a German Peace Garden was opened, and in 1990 an aviary added.

Address Kenilworth Road, CV3 6PT | Getting there 15-minute ride on the 12X or 10A bus from Pool Meadow station | Hours Unrestricted | Tip Each summer, the War Memorial park hosts the Coventry Godiva Festival, a 3-day music event that also offers family entertainment, food and drink, and a fun fair.

# 109  Warwick Arts Centre

*Head to the campus for Coventry's culture hub*

Warwick Arts Centre is the largest venue of its kind in the UK outside London, and is located within the University of Warwick's leafy campus in south Coventry. Opened in 1974, it has since welcomed more than 10 million visitors. Despite being at the centre of the university campus, most of those visiting for its major events are not students or academics, but local people from Coventry and Warwickshire, as well as visitors from further afield. The Arts Centre is open to the public, and every year attracts around 300,000 people to its busy performing and visual arts programme.

There are currently several venues inside the complex, including the 1,500 seat concert hall, the Butterworth Hall, two theatres – one seating up to 550 people, the other 150 – together with rehearsal rooms, a music centre, café and bar. Warwick Arts Centre's year-round programme includes art, music, drama, comedy, literature and film festivals, attracting some of the biggest names in modern entertainment in recent years – from Paul Weller to symphony orchestras, Jimmy Carr to Jeremy Irons. The centre also has its own commissioning and artist development programme. This provides artists with funds to give them time to develop their ideas, space in which to work, and an audience to engage with.

At the time of writing the Arts Centre is undergoing a major £27-million revamp, known as the Warwick 20:20 Project. Begun in 2017, the aim of the project is to create a new ground floor exhibition space, along with three cinemas and a brand new restaurant. There will also be a large new foyer, which will display and showcase contemporary art and sculpture, plus be a great place to meet up and relax with friends and family. Completion for the development work is planned for summer 2021, to coincide with the launch of Coventry's wide-ranging and long-planned UK City of Culture activities.

**Address** Warwick Arts Centre, University of Warwick, CV4 7AL, +44 (0)24 7652 4524, www.warwickartscentre.co.uk | Getting there 20-minute ride on the 12X or U12 bus from Pool Meadow station, or train to Canley Station and a 30-minute walk | Hours Check website for events | Tip While you're on campus, check out the industrial-looking, bright red *3B Series 1* sculpture, in the paved square between the Rootes Building and the Rootes residence – the first sculpture bought for the Warwick University campus, produced by Bernard Schottlander. Students call it 'TOIL', after the letter shapes of the forms that can be read from the residences.

# 110 Weaver's House

*Working from home 16th-century style*

Coventry's historic Spon Street is the location of six terraced cottages, built by the local Priory in 1455. Located just outside the original city wall, and featuring exposed cracked wooden beams, one of the cottages has been faithfully restored as an educational treat.

The aim of this restoration is to cast visitors back in time to give a glimpse into the everyday life of 16th-century loom-weaver John Croke and his family. It's a fascinating snapshot of social and economic history, illustrating what life would have been like for regular working-class citizens of the day. The intimate and personal nature of the showcase is a welcome contrast to the often detached nature of displays in other museums.

On open days, it's possible to tour this two-storey building, with volunteers providing fascinating commentary. The downstairs area features stone floors, exposed wooden beams, crumbling brickwork and tiny windows, where the family would live, eat and sleep. Visitors can learn about medieval building techniques, the kind of food the family would have eaten, plus the origins of phrases that have lasted centuries, such as 'true blue' after the work of the city's dyers, and 'sent to Coventry' (see ch. 78). A staircase and chimney added by later owners are also on show. Upstairs, accessed by a narrow ladder, is a working replica of the loom that would have been the source of the Croke family's income.

The cottage's medieval herb garden contains plants that would have been used to produce food and medicine, or for dyeing the material used in the loom a variety of different colours. On open days the scene is brought to life as volunteers engage in whittling, weeding, spinning wool or silk, and other 16th-century crafts, keeping alive those skills today. A Weavers' Workshop is also set up, giving visitors to Spon Street the opportunity to try their hand at different types of weaving themselves.

Address Upper Spon Street, CV1 3BQ, www.theweavershouse.org | Getting there 16-minute walk from Coventry railway station | Hours Check website for open days, always viewable from outside | Tip Coventry has a hidden river running through its heart! The Sherbourne was culverted beneath city centre developments in the 1960s. Visitors can see where it's channelled between the high rise flats of Spon End.

# 111 Ye Olde Saracen's Head

*Splendidly appointed specialist steak pub*

Ye Olde Saracen's Head in the village of Balsall Common, a couple of miles west of Coventry's boundary, is housed in a statuesque 16th-century building located in an area surrounded by beautiful West Midlands green belt countryside.

The pub is half-timbered, with a lovingly presented black and white frontage, diamond paned glass to the windows, and has been extended and renovated to a high standard in recent years. Known for many years for the wire sculptures of sheep on its front lawns, it all adds up to a bucolic slice of country pub life.

Part of the Marston's pub and brewery group, the Saracen's Head is geared towards restaurant-quality eating. There are wood-fired pizzas, and a fantastic steak menu offering a choice of the best quality cuts, such as rump, fillet, ribeye, sirloin and more. The Sunday roast is a big deal too. A good range of cask ales is on offer, plus a decent premium cocktails list. There are lots of nooks and corners that give groups of all sizes the sense they have their own space or snug in this welcoming environment, with exposed wooden beams and red brickwork. There's also a lovely wood-burning fire to cosy up to, while Bertie, a deer head with huge antlers mounted to the wall, surveys proceedings.

Out front, a 2020 revamp has added raised beds made from railway sleepers, which carry manicured shrubs that box in the front garden area. The pub's main entrance is at the back, from a generous car park, where there's now a large al fresco dining area under an awning-style canopy with outdoor heating, plus lots of space in a lovely beer garden with an abundance of benches. Ye Olde Saracen's Head is also popular with local dog walkers: canine companions are welcome in the bar area and beer garden, there's a figure of eight walk straight from the car park, and a dedicated dog feeding and watering station.

**Address** Balsall Street, Balsall Common, CV7 7AS, +44 (0)1676 533862, www.saracensheadbalsallcommon.com | **Getting there** Easiest by car, or a 30-minute walk from Berkswell railway station | **Hours** Daily midday–11pm | **Tip** A half-mile walk east down Balsall Street brings you to Oakes Farm Shop – it celebrates a field-to-fork ethos, with its on-site deli, café, butcher and baker.

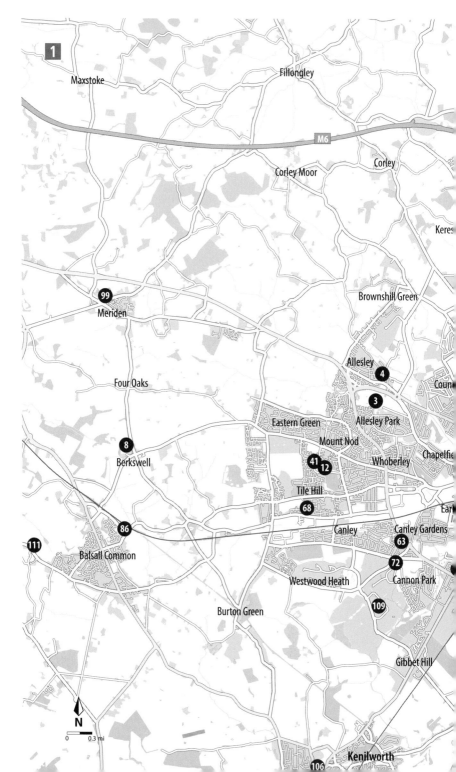

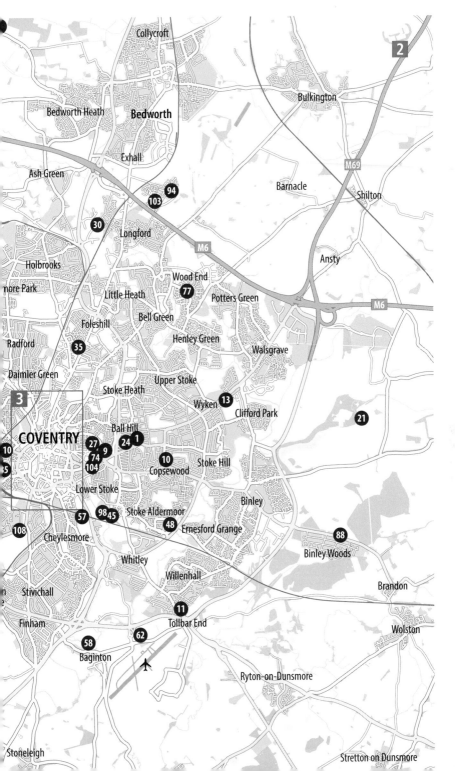

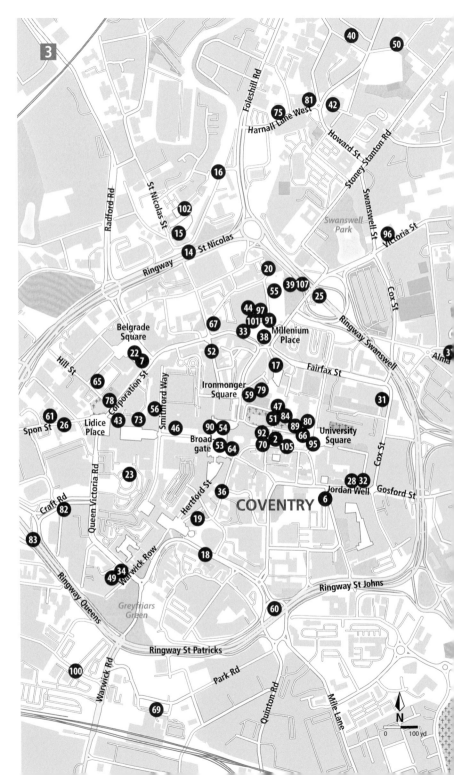

Martin Booth, Barbara Evripidou
**111 Places in Bristol
That You Shouldn't Miss**
ISBN 978-3-7408-0898-3

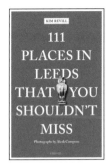

Kim Revill, Alesh Compton
**111 Places in Leeds
That You Shouldn't Miss**
ISBN 978-3-7408-0754-2

Julian Treuherz,
Peter de Figueiredo
**111 Places in Manchester
That You Shouldn't Miss**
ISBN 978-3-7408-0753-5

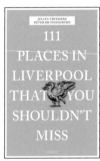

Julian Treuherz,
Peter de Figueiredo
**111 Places in Liverpool
That You Shouldn't Miss**
ISBN 978-3-95451-769-5

Michael Glover,
Richard Anderson
**111 Places in Sheffield
That You Shouldn't Miss**
ISBN 978-3-7408-0022-2

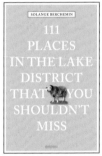

Solange Berchemin
**111 Places in the Lake District
That You Shouldn't Miss**
ISBN 978-3-7408-0378-0

John Sykes, Birgit Weber
**111 Places in London
That You Shouldn't Miss**
ISBN 978-3-95451-346-8

Nicola Perry, Daniel Reiter
**33 Walks in London
That You Shouldn't Miss**
ISBN 978-3-95451-886-9

Kirstin von Glasow
**111 Gardens in London
That You Shouldn't Miss**
ISBN 978-3-7408-0143-4

Laura Richards, Jamie Newson
**111 London Pubs and Bars
That You Shouldn't Miss**
ISBN 978-3-7408-0893-8

Emma Rose Barber,
Benedict Flett
**111 Churches in London
That You Shouldn't Miss**
ISBN 978-3-7408-0901-0

Ed Glinert, Marc Zakian
**111 Places in London's
East End That You
Shouldn't Miss**
ISBN 978-3-7408-0752-8

Katherine Bebo, Oliver Smith
**111 Places in Poole
That You Shouldn't Miss**
ISBN 978-3-7408-0598-2

Alexandra Loske
**111 Places in Brighton and
Lewes That You Shouldn't Miss**
ISBN 978-3-7408-0255-4

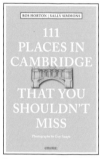

Rosalind Horton,
Sally Simmons, Guy Snape
**111 Places in Cambridge
That You Shouldn't Miss**
ISBN 978-3-7408-0147-2

Justin Postlethwaite
**111 Places in Bath
That You Shouldn't Miss**
ISBN 978-3-7408-0146-5

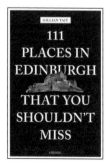

Gillian Tait
**111 Places in Edinburgh
That You Shouldn't Miss**
ISBN 978-3-95451-883-8

Tom Shields, Gillian Tait
**111 Places in Glasgow
That You Shouldn't Miss**
ISBN 978-3-7408-0256-1

Gillian Tait
**111 Places in Fife**
**That You Shouldn't Miss**
ISBN 978-3-7408-0597-5

Laszlo Trankovits
**111 Places in Jerusalem**
**That You Shouldn't Miss**
ISBN 978-3-7408-0320-9

Andrea Livnat,
Angelika Baumgartner
**111 Places in Tel Aviv**
**That You Shouldn't Miss**
ISBN 978-3-7408-0263-9

Alexia Amvrazi,
Diana Farr Louis, Diane Shugart,
Yannis Varouhakis
**111 Places in Athens**
**That You Shouldn't Miss**
ISBN 978-3-7408-0377-3

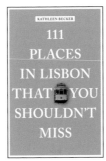

Kathleen Becker
**111 Places in Lisbon**
**That You Shouldn't Miss**
ISBN 978-3-7408-0383-4

Catrin George Ponciano
**111 Places along the Algarve**
**That You Shouldn't Miss**
ISBN 978-3-7408-0381-0

Thomas Fuchs
**111 Places in Amsterdam**
**That You Shouldn't Miss**
ISBN 978-3-7408-0023-9

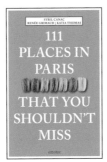

Sybil Canac, Renée Grimaud,
Katia Thomas
**111 Places in Paris**
**That You Shouldn't Miss**
ISBN 978-3-7408-0159-5

Matěj Černý, Marie Peřinová
**111 Places in Prague**
**That You Shouldn't Miss**
ISBN 978-3-7408-0144-1

Jan Gralle, Vibe Skytte,
Kurt Rodahl Hoppe
**111 Places in Copenhagen
That You Shouldn't Miss**
ISBN 978-3-7408-0580-7

Kai Oidtmann
**111 Places in Iceland
That You Shouldn't Miss**
ISBN 978-3-7408-0030-7

Jo-Anne Elikann
**111 Places in New York
That You Must Not Miss**
ISBN 978-3-95451-052-8

Floriana Petersen, Steve Werney
**111 Places in San Francisco
That You Must Not Miss**
ISBN 978-3-95451-609-4

Laurel Moglen, Julia Posey,
Lyudmila Zotova
**111 Places in Los Angeles
That You Must Not Miss**
ISBN 978-3-95451-884-5

Amy Bizzarri, Susie Inverso
**111 Places in Chicago
That You Must Not Miss**
ISBN 978-3-7408-1030-6

Dave Doroghy, Graeme Menzies
**111 Places in Vancouver
That You Must Not Miss**
ISBN 978-3-7408-0494-7

Anita Mai Genua,
Clare Davenport,
Elizabeth Lenell Davies
**111 Places in Toronto
That You Must Not Miss**
ISBN 978-3-7408-0257-8

Jennifer Bain, Christina Ryan
**111 Places in Calgary
That You Must Not Miss**
ISBN 978-3-7408-0749-8

*Acknowledgements*

My Mum and Dad have lived all their lives in Coventry, and I'm grateful they raised me in such a vibrant and historic city. Thanks to them, and to my brother and oldest Cov mates, for suggesting many of the storied places that populate these pages.

Once I started compiling a list for this book, I couldn't get enough of discovering my hometown all over again. I raced through the excellent books of Coventry historian David McGrory, Rob Orland's encyclopaedic Historic Coventry, the wonderful Coventry Society website and many more sources.

Lots of people helped me a great deal with this book, but special thanks to Paul Jones and Julie Fairbrother at Coventry City Council, James Gorry at Coventry City of Culture Trust, and Jonathan Davidson at Writing West Midlands.

Thanks to all the many people who were generous with their time and energies in showing me what makes Coventry so exciting today, and why it richly deserves its status as UK City of Culture 2021.

Thanks to Laura Olk and Martin Sketchley for all your support, and finally to Ian Williams for the wonderful images you've captured – I'm proud of what we've achieved and hope these 111 Places reflect the spirit and exuberance of Coventry.

**Rob Ganley** was born and raised in Coventry, before following a publishing career in London. He has been a magazine writer and editor for more than 20 years, and also writes fiction. Today he lives in Rugby, just outside Coventry where many of his family remain, and enjoys watching it change and evolve at exhilarating speed.

**Ian Williams**, born and raised in the North East of England and although now living happily in the south, still considers himself to be at heart a northern lad. Photography found Ian at an early age, hooking him into developing and printing grainy images shot on his 127 Brownie. Since those formative days a camera has not been far from his hand. A lifetime later, Ian continues to refine his craft, whether shooting Interiors for clients or wild landscapes for personal satisfaction his quest for the perfect shot continues.